How (not) to Do It All

Dr Emma Short is a Consultant NHS doctor specialising in histopathology. She studied pre-clinical medicine at Cambridge University and clinical medicine at Oxford University. She completed her basic surgical training in Devon, before moving to Wales for her histopathology training. Emma also has a PhD from Cardiff University in cancer genetics and is a health and fitness writer.

How (not) to Do It All

Energise Your Life

Dr Emma Short

Parthian, Cardigan SA43 1ED
www.parthianbooks.com
First published in 2023
© Dr Emma Short 2023
ISBN Paperback: 978-1-914595-38-7
ISBN eBook: 978-1-914595-39-4
Editor:
Cover design
Typeset by Elaine Sharples
Printed and bound by 4edge Limited, UK
Published with the financial support of the Welsh Books Council
British Library Cataloguing in Publication Data
A cataloguing record for this book is available from the British Library.

Contents

Welcome

Hello, I'm Dr Emma Short and I work as a consultant histopathologist in the NHS. I'm the type of doctor who diagnoses diseases by examining tiny pieces of tissue under the microscope. I also have a PhD in cancer genetics – I spent five years looking into the reasons why some people are genetically predisposed to developing multiple polyps in their bowel. Polyps are minute growths which usually just sit in the intestines and go unnoticed, but a small proportion of polyps develop into bowel cancer.

So why am I writing a book about lifestyle changes to improve health and wellbeing when I don't have direct contact with patients? It is because my work led me to look at how people can improve their health to prevent disease.

A large part of my clinical work involves diagnosing cancer. Cancer cells look ugly under the microscope ... instead of being neat, orderly and uniform, they are random in size and shape. They're often crowded and jumbled and don't respect each other's boundaries. Cancer cells grow in an uncontrolled manner and they don't stay where they're supposed to be. They invade healthy tissue and try to enter blood vessels or lymphatic channels so they can spread to other parts of the body. During my PhD, I spent many hours at cancer-related conferences, and it was clear that vast amounts of research time and money are spent on the diagnosis of cancer and its treatment. This is vitally important, but significantly fewer resources are spent on health promotion and cancer prevention. Surely 'prevention is better than cure'? Data shows that up to fifty per cent of cancers could be avoided.

Cancer follows heart disease and stroke as the biggest killer in the developed world. When it comes to heart disease, we know that eighty per cent of premature heart disease, along with stroke and type 2 diabetes, can be prevented through changes in lifestyle.

I qualified as a personal trainer to get a better understanding of the impact that exercise and movement can have on our health. I also trained as a meditation teacher and completed diplomas in mindful nutrition and forest bathing, to appreciate the beneficial effects of a holistic approach to healthcare.

Lifestyle changes don't need to be complicated, time-consuming or expensive. Significant improvements can be achieved through simple measures such as being physically active, minimising the time spent sitting down, eating a healthy and balanced diet, maintaining a healthy weight, not smoking, moderating alcohol intake and maintaining social relationships. This approach to healthcare, known as Lifestyle Medicine, is gaining popularity all over the world.

I feel so strongly about the positive effects of lifestyle changes that I compiled a textbook for healthcare professionals, which was published in 2021. It includes the latest scientific knowledge and is called *A Prescription for Healthy Living: A Guide to Lifestyle Medicine* (Elsevier, 2021). It aims to inspire and encourage doctors to empower their patients to make behavioural changes to improve their health.

But I really want to make this information available to everybody, not just the professionals. I want everyone to have the knowledge and skillset to take control of their lifestyle, so they feel healthier, happier and energised.

That is where this book comes in. It contains information, advice and tips to improve your wellbeing and it includes contributions from other doctors and healthcare professionals who are also passionate about a holistic approach to improving health.

Traditionally, there are six pillars of Lifestyle Medicine. These are physical activity, optimising nutrition, stress reduction, social connectivity, optimising sleep and reducing the use of harmful substances. I like to use the acronym ENERGISE™ to explore how these areas can be incorporated into your everyday lives. ENERGISE™ stands for:

Exercise and Movement
Nutrition
Environment
Relationships and social connections
Goal setting and habits
Ideas, mindset and stress reduction
Sleep
Empower

This book has a chapter on each of these topics. Don't feel you have to read the book from cover to cover, dip in and learn more about the areas which appeal to you. One of the great things about lifestyle interventions is that small changes can often have a huge impact. For example, studies have reported that if we sit for periods of less than thirty minutes at a time, we have a fifty-five per cent lower risk of death than those who sit for more than thirty minutes. This suggests we can improve our life span by just moving more regularly.

If we make a conscious effort to make one small change every day, we will soon feel a positive impact on our wellbeing. For example, if we want to focus on our nutrition, we could swap a biscuit for a banana, a can of coke for water or a piece of cake for yoghurt. Similarly, if we choose to improve how much we move, we could use the stairs rather than a lift, or we could decide not to park in the space nearest the shops in favour of one further away. These small changes will soon make a big difference to how you feel, which will strengthen your motivation and enthusiasm to make even more changes.

A fantastic aspect of adopting healthy behaviours is that one action often has a positive effect on multiple other areas. For example, going for a run with a friend gives you the benefit of exercise and also reduces your stress levels, helps your social connections, improves your sleep and gives you time in nature. If you cook a healthy meal for your family, you can share good nutrition, strengthen family ties and you're not being sedentary while you're standing chopping and dicing.

Another strategy I'd strongly recommend at the start of your wellness journey is to **immediately see yourself as a healthy person**. Our sense of identity describes how we view ourselves. This is the result of a complex interplay of factors including our life experiences, our achievements, the challenges we have faced, our values and our views of the world.

Importantly, how we see ourselves affects our behaviour. If we identify as being healthy, we are more likely to make healthy choices. Even if we don't initially feel that we are healthy or fit, telling ourselves that we are makes changes easier and more sustainable.

I hope you enjoy this book and enjoy making lifestyle choices that make you feel healthier and happier. I'd love to hear how you get on and what works for you!

@dr_emmashort
The Healthy Happy Gut Doctor
www.energisehealth.org

Disclaimer: this book is a guide to lifestyle changes that can be made to improve health and wellbeing. It doesn't replace any advice you have been given from your own doctor or healthcare professional. If you have any health concerns, please talk to your relevant healthcare provider.

Exercise and Movement
Dr Emma Short and Dr Caroline Deodhar

Exercise and movement are, by far, my favourite lifestyle interventions to improve health and wellbeing. I love running and being outside in nature, and it is through running that I have met many of my closest friends. I also enjoy yoga and body combat and one of our favourite family activities is a walk by our local river. The benefits of exercise are immediately apparent – you feel great and it gives you a mental boost that lasts all day long.

What is exercise?

Exercise describes any activity which causes us to exert ourselves physically. It's broadly divided into three categories – cardiovascular exercise, strength work and flexibility. Cardiovascular exercise makes our breathing rate increase and our heart pump faster. We traditionally think of cardiovascular exercise as sports such as running, football, dancing or hockey, but actually everyday activities such as gardening and vigorous housework also count. Similarly, strength work doesn't just mean lifting weights at the gym. When we're carrying heavy shopping bags or pushing a full wheelbarrow, that's building our strength too.

Inadequate levels of exercise are a major risk factor for chronic disease and premature death. Middle-aged women who complete less than one hour of physical activity a week have a doubled risk of death compared to those who exercise regularly. To put this into context, these figures are similar to the increase in risk caused by moderate cigarette smoking.

What happens when we exercise?

When we exercise, our bodies need to work to increase the delivery of oxygen and nutrients to our muscles so they can produce energy. This is why our heart rate and breathing rate increase. With continued and regular activity, our bodies adapt so they can work more efficiently.

Some of the changes which occur include our hearts becoming stronger and pumping more blood with each beat, and our muscles increasing in size and producing energy more effectively. There is also improved elimination of waste products, enhanced gas exchange in the lungs and a healthier profile of lipids in the blood. Additional benefits include improved control of blood sugar levels and reduced inflammation throughout the body. Inflammation is a vital and necessary part of our body's response to a harmful stimulus, such as an infection or an injury. For example, if we cut our skin, the area around the wound becomes red, warm, swollen and tender. This happens because our blood vessels dilate to deliver inflammatory cells and chemical messengers to the site of injury in order to start the repair and healing process. In this context, the inflammatory process is said to be 'acute' as it occurs in response to a specific event and it only lasts for a short time period. 'Chronic inflammation' describes inflammation which lasts longer, from weeks to months to years. Different inflammatory cells and different chemical messengers are involved, and the inflammation can occur throughout the body. Chronic inflammation is associated with a variety of diseases, including diabetes, heart disease, cancer and Alzheimer's. Lifestyle factors such as smoking, alcohol consumption, stress and obesity may all contribute to the development and ongoing activity of chronic inflammation.

What are the health benefits of exercise?

Exercise and being active have a myriad of benefits, not just for our physical health but for our mental health and wellbeing too. If we are physically active, our risk of death from any cause is reduced by around fifty per cent compared to those people who are inactive. Generally, the fitter we become, the greater the reduction in risk. Exercise reduces the risk of developing cardiovascular disease by thirty-five per cent and is also good for those who already have a diagnosis of established heart disease. Studies show that physical activity can slow the progression of coronary artery disease – the 'furring up' of the blood vessels that supply the heart. Exercise reduces the risk of developing type 2 diabetes by forty per cent and reduces the risk of death for anyone who already has type 2 diabetes. Regular activity can also reduce blood pressure, especially for those with mild and moderate hypertension. For some people, this can be enough to allow them to come off medication.

If all that isn't enough incentive, exercise can also reduce the likelihood of developing cancer, particularly breast and bowel cancer, and has been proven to improve outcomes for people who have already been diagnosed with breast cancer. Studies have shown that moderate exercise can reduce the risk of breast cancer recurring and can reduce the risk of death from breast cancer, especially in certain tumour types.

Exercise reduces the risk of falls, depression and dementia by thirty per cent and joint and back pain by twenty-five per cent. Exercise is also an important tool in maintaining a healthy weight, as we burn more calories when we are active.

Improving our mood
Exercise has significant and positive effects on our mood and can reduce symptoms of anxiety and depression. Positive effects can be observed in a relatively short time frame – individuals diagnosed with a major depressive episode were found to have a significant reduction in depression after a daily exercise session of thirty minutes, which they carried out over a ten-day period.

I know the fantastic effects that exercise has on my mood – if ever I'm feeling bad-tempered or 'down', a run will always lift my spirits. When we exercise, our bodies release chemicals called endorphins. These are similar in structure to morphine, and make us feel positive and energised, and can also reduce our perception of pain.

Exercise can improve both the quality and duration of sleep, which in turn will have a positive impact on mood, overall health and wellbeing. It's best to do exercise outside and early in the day for it to have its maximum positive effect on sleep.

Lorraine, IT manager, age 52

As I was growing up, and during my adult years, I have suffered from periods of low mood and depression. In the last thirteen years, I have lost both my dad and a daughter. It can be really hard to deal with life's challenges. I have, however, found that exercise has a hugely positive impact on my health and wellbeing. Running helps to keep me positive. I have always found it difficult to 'switch off' and sleep, but regular exercise helps to calm my mind. I am blessed with having a local park and river near where I live. This is my 'go to' place for running when I am stressed, and I feel a connection with nature when I exercise outside near the trees and water. I like to exercise with friends and talking helps me to feel resilient.

Healthy bones

Our bones are living tissues and they increase in mass until we're around the age of thirty years. There are many things that can affect our bone health including hormones, diet and sun exposure. Exercise is really important in helping our bones to achieve their optimal mass. Bones will respond to forces placed upon them by becoming stronger. If children and teenagers stay active and do regular weight-bearing activities such as walking, jogging, dancing or playing tennis, this will improve bone strength. Activity during adolescence has been shown to directly reduce the risk of developing osteoporosis, or weak and fragile bones, in older age. As we move into adulthood, exercise, particularly weight-bearing exercise, is important in reducing the rate of loss of bone mass and therefore reducing the risk of osteoporosis.

Enhance our brain power

Our cognitive function often declines as we age. High levels of physical activity have been shown to protect against cognitive impairment. In addition to this, exercise may also reduce the risk of developing Alzheimer's Disease.

> **Lucy, doctor, age 41**
> *Exercise is a hugely important part of my life, but I haven't always had a positive relationship with it.*
>
> *As a child and teenager, I was very sporty. I was active, I ate what I wanted and I was confident in my appearance. I also studied hard and went to university to study medicine. As a medical student, I was a member of the gymnastics club and the football team ... I even avoided alcohol on the day we got our final exam results as I had a gymnastics competition the following morning!*
>
> *Starting work as a junior doctor was a shock to the system. Long hours, night shifts and weekend work made it difficult to stick to a routine and everything slipped. Gradually, I stopped doing any exercise, I stopped looking after myself and I became accustomed to sitting on my sofa. As I got more senior at work, I had exams to study for. I got married and had children and my own health was never my priority. On a few occasions, I tried to go to the gym, but it wasn't something I enjoyed, and I resented 'having' to go.*
>
> *After a few years, I wasn't in a good place. I was struggling to balance work and family life and found myself failing my exams. I had gained weight, lost confidence in myself and I felt*

I was stuck in a rut. I was supported by my workplace, which offered me sessions with a coach. Through my coach I explored my goals and my ideas about myself. Something my coach said will always resonate with me: 'If you don't like something, change it.' It sounds simple, but it really empowered me. I bought some new clothes that made me feel good, I started to take better care of my skin, and I thought about starting to exercise again. I looked at what options were available, but I always found an excuse not to begin.

One night I was sitting in my usual spot on my sofa, browsing my phone, and I saw an advert for a new kind of class. The class was in a darkened room, with glowsticks and disco lights. This really appealed to me – no one would see how unfit I was or how I could no longer comfortably fit into a leotard. After a glass of wine, I booked and paid for my place. I was going to do this.

On the day of the class, I drove to the venue dressed in black and full of dread. I was physically shaking with nerves, and my inner voice was telling me I couldn't do it. However, I managed to find the courage to walk into the building, pick up my glowsticks and find my place right at the back of the hall.

I can't explain the euphoria I felt as the music started and everyone started to move. The sweat poured and my spirits lifted. I am sure I walked taller out of the hall that day. I got home and booked on again for the following week.

Week after week I went to class. I started to move closer to the front, wear brighter colours, whoop along and my smile got bigger and bigger. One day my instructor asked if I wanted to come on the stage and dance next to her. When I saw all those faces looking back at me, I felt a sense of belonging. My physical health was in a better place, my mental health was in a better place and my confidence was shining through in all aspects of my life.

I had a lightbulb moment – what if I could help people to feel the way about exercise that I now felt? I wanted to help others to overcome their doubts and to experience the joy that I experience. I have now trained as a fitness instructor and, although it can be tricky balancing work, family life and my fitness business, I wouldn't have it any other way.

How much exercise should I be doing?

The current government recommendations are that adults should spend one hundred and fifty minutes every week doing moderate-intensity aerobic activity, or seventy-five minutes doing vigorous activity, or a mixture of both.

Aerobic activity describes the activities which increase the heart rate and breathing rate – exercises like walking, jogging and cycling. A good way to gauge the intensity of exercise is whether you're able to talk. With moderate intensity, you can speak in short sentences but you couldn't sing a song, whereas with vigorous intense activity you can only say a couple of words at a time.

It's good to split the one hundred and fifty minutes so you do thirty minutes over five days. It can be achieved in bouts of ten minutes, so you don't have to do too much in any one go.

The number of adults who achieve this level of activity in the UK is low. The British Heart Foundation reports that around thirty-nine per cent of UK adults are failing to meet government recommendations for physical activity. This equals about twenty million people. The statistics are worse for women than men – nearly twelve million women across the UK are not active enough compared to around eight million men. Overall, women are thirty-six per cent more likely to be classified as physically inactive.

If you're thinking about doing more exercise, it can be helpful to ask yourself what any potential barriers might be, and ways you could overcome them. Some common examples and potential solutions are listed below:

BARRIER	SOLUTION
Not enough time	You don't need to do a whole exercise class – the benefits of being active can be seen with short ten-minute sessions.
	Try 'exercise snacking' – incorporate a ten-minute activity as often as you can throughout the day. You could get up slightly earlier to go for a run, walk during your lunch break or jog on the spot whilst you're watching the television.
	Instead of saying 'I haven't got enough time to exercise', say 'I'm going to prioritise exercise' – this can be a helpful way to shift your mindset. Is there anything you currently do that could be swapped for physical activity?
Not enough money	Many activities are free to do, for example, walking and running. There are also many free online workouts available, and several fitness centres offer free classes for anyone with a low income.
	Trainers can be bought second-hand, and there are a few charities that provide free sportswear.
Feeling too tired	The great thing about exercise is that it gives us more energy! If we're not active, we can enter a vicious cycle of feeling too tired to exercise, being sedentary, then feeling even more tired.
	If you're worn out by the end of the day, try exercising first thing in the morning, or during your lunch break, or you could go to the gym on your way home from work before you crash on the sofa. Once you start to be active regularly, you may well be surprised by how much more energy, drive and motivation you have.

BARRIER	SOLUTION
Not enough confidence	Unfortunately, it is incredibly common to hear that people don't want to exercise because they don't feel confident enough to do so. They often feel that they will be judged by others because of how unfit they are or because of how they look.
	Try not to focus on other people and their opinions. It really doesn't matter, and the likelihood is that they feel exactly the same way as you do, or they're so occupied by their own workout that they won't even notice you.
	If you don't like to exercise with many other people around, you could start with home workouts, or go to the gym at the off-peak times. Alternatively, some people find that they'd rather exercise with several friends, as being part of a group gives support and encouragement, and there is less of a spotlight on any one individual.
	It can be helpful to recognise and celebrate what your body can do and how it is becoming fitter and healthier. For example, notice and be proud when you're able to run for a minute when previously it was thirty seconds, or when you can lift twenty kilograms rather than a starting weight of five kilograms.
	Focus on your end goal. Always keep in mind your why – you're moving more to feel healthier, happier, fitter, stronger and more energised.
Finding exercise boring	There are so many different ways to stay active, and it's really important to find the way that you enjoy so that exercise is a pleasure and not a chore. Some people fall in love with one sport, others like a variety of different activities.

Strength and flexibility are important too!

Aerobic activities are what most of us think of when we talk about exercising, but it's also really important to work on our strength and flexibility.

Resistance training, or strength training, describes exercises that cause our muscles to work hard so they maintain or increase their size and become stronger or more powerful. Our muscles allow us to move, and they are also important in protein and energy metabolism. Our muscle mass declines by up to eight per cent every decade after the age of thirty, and by up to ten per cent every decade after the age of fifty. This loss in muscle mass is associated with a reduction in our basal metabolic rate, which can lead to fat gain. It also increases our risk of falls and fractures, slows our recovery from illness and wound healing, increases the likelihood of physical disability and worsens our quality of life.

Strength training helps us to maintain or improve our muscle mass, which reduces the risk of the adverse outcomes described above. It has many additional benefits, including weight control, reducing back pain, reducing the risk of osteoporosis and helping with the regulation of our blood sugar levels.

It is recommended that adults should do activities that strengthen the major muscle groups at least two days a week. This can be done using weights in a gym but can just as easily be done at home using our own body weight, resistance bands, or even doing activities such as carrying heavy shopping or heavy gardening.

As well as strength work, it is also recommended that adults should do exercises that maintain or enhance their flexibility at least twice a week.

Flexibility can be thought of as the range of movement we have at our joints. As we get older, our flexibility decreases, which is largely due to a reduction in physical activity levels, along with changes that occur within our joints and tissues. It is important to try and maintain our flexibility so that we don't 'stiffen up' with age. Being flexible improves our balance, mobility, posture and muscle coordination, and reduces our risk of injury. Activities such as yoga and Pilates are good for flexibility, but simple stretches will also do the trick. If you're stretching at home, it's important that you have warmed up your muscles first. An ideal time to stretch is in the cool-down period after an aerobic activity.

My personal exercise story

I was never an athletic child or teenager. I went to dancing classes when I was at primary school, but I stopped these when a dance show and its preceding rehearsals clashed with a chess tournament and the chess club meetings. Throughout my school and university years, my main priority was my academic studies. Exercise and fitness weren't even on my radar. As a newly qualified doctor, I went for an extremely rare run, but this was never something I did regularly or considered to be important.

When we moved to Wales, my next-door neighbour, Lou, who is now one of my closest friends, was often out running or heading to the gym. She encouraged me to join her and was extremely patient and supportive as I slowly plodded next to her. One evening in 2017, after a few glasses of wine and a curry, we set ourselves a target of running a half-marathon. From that moment onwards, running became a huge part of my life.

We signed up to do the Cardiff half-marathon, which would take place seven months later. At that time, I didn't really know anything at all about exercise. I wrote my own training schedule, which simply involved three runs a week – a short run, a middle-distance run and a long run, which would increase by one kilometre every week. My long runs were fuelled by porridge or peanut butter and jam on toast, and I ate jelly babies as I ran. After three months I was able to run 20 km, so I decided not to wait for the Cardiff half and completed the Swansea half instead, as that was held four months earlier. I loved every minute.

Since then I have spent many, many hours reading about exercise physiology, training schedules, sports nutrition, hydration and recovery techniques. I have qualified as a run leader, fitness instructor and personal trainer – largely because of the enjoyment and pleasure I get from learning about exercise and movement. I love using this knowledge to help other people to improve their own health and wellbeing. I set up a local running club, and I find it incredible to share the joy of running with others and to see them grow in confidence and self-belief.

Over the years I've run many races – from 5 km to ultra-marathons. I enjoy the buzz and energy of race days, and I like having a goal to aim for, but speed isn't important to me. A marathon is a marathon if you run it in three hours or six hours. At the moment I'm enjoying running for running's sake. I haven't got a race booked in, so I'm taking great pleasure in running for what it is – an opportunity to be outside in nature and to feel healthy and strong. During a typical week, I try to run three or four times, and I also like to include a high-intensity interval training (HIIT) or strength session and a combat class at the gym.

For me, keeping healthy through fitness and exercise has become a really important part of who I am. Running makes me happy and energised, and if I've run early in the morning, I feel like I've achieved something before the day has begun. I also find that running gives me the headspace to think about anything on my mind – it's often when I'm running that I find solutions to problems or plan the next stages of the projects I'm involved in.

Another benefit of exercise is that it helps my sleep – if I've had a sedentary day, it's hard for me to drop off at night. In addition, it's through exercise that I've learned to love my body. I may have a wobbly tummy and cellulite on my thighs, but this body can run for hours on end and allows me to do what I love.

The final huge plus of exercise, for me, is the community you become a part of. I have met many of my closest friends through running, and we spend hours putting the world to rights during our weekend outings.

What is high-intensity interval training (HIIT) and why is it so popular?

High-intensity interval training – or HIIT for short – has become increasingly popular over the last few years. It involves short, intense bursts of activity with recovery periods in between. HIIT has got a reputation for being an extremely time-efficient way to exercise. Fans of HIIT claim it improves cardiovascular fitness and boosts your metabolic rate so you continue to burn fat even when your workout is complete. An added bonus is that a HIIT session can be done anywhere, at any time, so you don't need to travel to a gym to train.

How does HIIT work?

We need to understand how our bodies generate energy during exercise to understand how HIIT training works. There are three energy systems at play when we are active – these are the creatine phosphate system, the aerobic energy system and the anaerobic energy system. All of these have a role to play in generating a molecule called adenosine triphosphate, or ATP, which is the energy currency that our bodies need for it to function.

The creatine phosphate system gives us a short, sharp burst of energy which lasts for about ten to fifteen seconds. This is the main energy system used in sports such as high jump or javelin. This system can provide immediate bursts of energy, as it uses ATP which is already present in the muscles and it generates ATP from the breakdown of another substance, phosphocreatine. However, this supply of ATP is very short-lived and it needs to be regenerated.

When we exercise for a long time at a low-moderate pace, we primarily use the aerobic energy system. It is called 'aerobic' because it requires oxygen. Fatty acids and glucose are broken down to give us energy, and the waste products are carbon dioxide and water, which the body can easily get rid of.

When we do a HIIT session, we are working so hard that we can't get enough oxygen to our muscles to meet their demands for the aerobic energy system. When this happens, the body is still able to use glucose for energy, but it does so anaerobically, in other words without oxygen. The waste product in this case is lactic acid. When lactic acid builds up in our muscles, we experience a burning sensation and we rapidly tire so we can't carry on exercising at high intensity.

HIIT training has been shown to increase our VO_2 max, which is a way of measuring our aerobic fitness. It considers how efficiently our hearts, lungs, circulation and muscles take in and use oxygen during exercise. When our VO_2 max increases, there is more oxygen available to our muscles. This means that we can carry on using the aerobic energy system for longer – our lactate threshold has increased so we can work harder for a greater duration. Another plus is that HIIT enhances the clearance of lactic acid, so the body gets rid of it more efficiently. HIIT training has also been shown to upregulate enzymes involved in both aerobic and anaerobic metabolism, which improves the availability of energy in working muscles.

In a nutshell, this all means that we get fitter.

HIIT isn't just beneficial for healthy individuals. A research group in Australia reviewed several studies that had considered the effects of HIIT workouts in patients with heart disease, high blood pressure, metabolic syndrome and obesity. In these patients, HIIT improved VO_2 max to a greater extent than moderate-intensity continuous training, indicating that their cardiorespiratory fitness had improved. In addition to the improvement in VO_2 max, patients demonstrated improved blood pressure readings, improved lipid profiles in their blood, increased enjoyment of exercise and improved quality of life.

Don't overdo it

Whilst HIIT training has many benefits, it doesn't come without risks. Because you are working at a high intensity, you are at risk of overtraining. Your body needs time to recover and adapt after a hard workout. Different fitness experts have different recommendations as to what should be the maximum number of HIIT sessions you do in a week, and this will depend on how hard you push yourself during a session. My personal feeling is that two HIIT workouts a week should be the upper limit. This could involve doing sprint intervals whilst running or cycling, or a routine at home, for example, thirty seconds on/thirty seconds' rest of exercises such as star jumps, burpees, mountain climbers or tuck jumps.

Sit less, move more

As well as being physically active, it is also important not to spend too much time sitting, as sedentary behaviour is a risk factor in itself for developing chronic disease. It's possible that someone could meet their exercise targets over the course of a week, but they could still be thought of as sedentary if the rest of their time is spent sitting down. Sedentary behaviour describes sitting or lying whilst not doing much else, and it includes watching television, working at the computer, driving, listening to music or reading. It is reported that adults currently spend between nine and ten hours every day sitting, and more than four in ten adults in the UK do not even manage to achieve ten minutes of brisk continuous walking over a month.

We have been aware of the dangers of sedentary behaviour for over half a century. In the 1950s there was a famous London Transport Workers Study which reported that the bus drivers, who sat down all day, had much higher rates of heart disease than the bus conductors, who spent their time at work standing. If the conductors did develop heart disease, it was at a later age than the drivers and was less likely to be fatal.

Since that time, many studies have shown that sedentary behaviour is associated with symptoms of depression and anxiety, type 2 diabetes, heart disease, certain cancers and an increased risk of premature death. The statistics associated with the health risks of sedentary behaviour are really quite dramatic, for example, individuals who sit for more than thirteen hours a day have a two hundred per cent greater risk of death than those who sit for less than approximately eleven hours a day. Those who sit for stretches of less than thirty minutes have a fifty-five per cent lower risk of death than those who sit for more than thirty minutes. If we want to negate the risks of sitting we really need to work hard – we would need to complete sixty to seventy-five minutes of moderate-intensity activity every day, and if we watch television for five or more hours a day even this level of activity would not completely eliminate the health risks.

Although there aren't formal guidelines about how often we should move, the key advice is to **sit less, move more**.

How to be more active

The most important thing is to exercise safely. If you have any pre-existing health conditions, it is advised you speak to your GP or healthcare provider before starting to exercise. Some areas offer exercise referral schemes which are classes designed for specific groups of people, for example, anyone who has had a cancer diagnosis or those with fibromyalgia.

The hardest step is often to start a new fitness regime. Try to find an activity that you enjoy doing and set yourself SMART goals, which are Specific, Measurable, Achievable, Realistic and Time-bound. Goal setting will be explored in detail later in this book. You could start by committing to walk one mile during your lunch break every day for four weeks. Goals can enhance motivation and commitment to an exercise programme and you can adapt your goals as you progress and your fitness levels improve. It's important not to overwhelm yourself when you first set out. This is essential to both maintain motivation and to avoid injury. Take things gently and increase your exercise intensity and duration gradually.

Exercise doesn't have to be done in a gym. What really matters is increasing your general activity levels, so it's fantastic if you can incorporate being active into your daily life. Try getting off the bus or the train a stop earlier, cycling to work, taking a walk during your tea break, always using the stairs rather than the lift, doing your housework with vigour or taking up gardening.

If you own a smartphone, there are several free or low-cost apps which provide workout plans and guidance. One of the most popular programs is the 'Couch to 5K' plan, which is endorsed by the NHS and is an excellent way for those new to physical activity to access the world of running.

Many leisure centres offer a variety of classes if you prefer to work out as part of a group. These can range from boxing classes to Zumba, and they have additional social benefits as you meet other like-minded people. Training buddies can be a great motivation! If you've made plans to meet someone to do an activity, you often find you're more likely to stick to it as you don't want to let them down.

Some people find it best if they exercise first thing in the morning. It's then done for the day, so you can't use 'being tired after work' as an excuse and you get an early morning endorphin rush so start the day with a bang! If you're going to work out in the evening, change into your sportswear as soon as you get in from work. That way you're already getting into the mindset of doing exercise and are more likely to see it through.

To reduce periods of sedentary time it can be helpful to set an alarm to go off at regular intervals to prompt you to move. Many smartwatches include a feature where they buzz every hour to encourage you to stand up and move, and this can be quite an effective motivator for some people. If you work at a desk, consider an under-the-desk device such as a bike or pedal-pusher, or even swap your seated desk to a standing desk. When you get up to go to the toilet, choose the bathroom furthest away, and when you need to throw something away, get up to go to the bin. When you're making a cup of tea, try doing some squats whilst waiting for the kettle to boil and when you're watching the television, consider standing rather than sitting – you could combine it with ironing or you could practise some stretches. Most of us spend a lot of time using our mobile phones – aim to walk and talk.

A good tip is never to compare yourself to other people. If you want to make any comparisons, compare your active self to the old you who didn't exercise or who spent a lot of time sitting. It's almost guaranteed that you will feel happier, have more energy, have more self-confidence and have an improved overall sense of wellbeing.

OPTIONAL CHALLENGES:

- Over the next week, aim to increase your physical activity levels. This could be a small change, for example, hoovering on alternate days if you usually do it once a week. Or you could aim for a bigger goal, for example, getting up half an hour earlier on two days to go for an early-morning walk.
- When you talk on your mobile phone, don't sit down – if possible, try to walk up and down the room as you talk.
- Consider how you can build more movement into your working day, taking into account your working environment. Are there small tweaks you can make so that you're moving every hour?
- Think about your commute and if there are any ways you could use this to be more active. Could you get off the bus a stop early, bike to work instead of drive or take the bus to work and walk home?

Nutrition, Healthy Eating, Weight and the Gut Microbiome

A healthy and balanced diet is a fundamental aspect of health and wellbeing. The food we eat, when we eat and how much we eat, is vitally important in determining our risk of developing obesity, heart disease, stroke, type 2 diabetes and certain cancers. It can also affect the severity of symptoms in a range of chronic diseases such as inflammatory bowel disease and depression.

However, the subject of diet is highly emotive, and the most effective eating pattern is hotly debated across the fields of science, nutrition and medicine. Food is primarily a fuel for our bodies, but the way we eat is affected by a wide range of factors including social, cultural, ethical, medical and religious influences. Add to that the fact that we don't eat only when we are hungry or to nourish our bodies. We may eat for pleasure or because we are tired, bored, stressed, lonely, angry, as a habit, or for a multitude of other reasons.

I am not going to advocate a specific diet or eating pattern. This is because I believe that different diets work for different people, depending on many factors such as age, gender, activity levels, overall health, beliefs, finances and lifestyle.

It is important that every individual finds a healthy diet which works for them. We want healthy choices to be sustainable in the long term, and not to take the joy out of food. So, I will explore the general principles of healthy eating, along with the importance of maintaining a healthy weight and the gut microbiome.

The principles of healthy eating

A healthy and balanced diet feeds our body and mind. It can reduce the risk of developing certain diseases and it impacts our mood. Research has shown that most people in the UK aren't meeting the recommended standards for healthy eating. Generally, we are consuming too much sugar, salt and saturated fat and we aren't eating enough fruit, vegetables and fibre.

Macronutrients, micronutrients and fibre

What is a 'balanced diet'? It is one which includes proteins, carbohydrates and fats (macronutrients) as well as vitamins and minerals (micronutrients).

Macronutrients

Macronutrients make up the bulk of our food intake and have a variety of roles in our bodies. Proteins play a major part in growth and repair, they're part of our muscle make-up and they have many other functions, for example, as enzymes and antibodies.

Carbohydrates are our body's preferred energy source and are also incredibly important as fibre. We need fibre to keep our bowels moving. Not only that, it can reduce our risk of heart disease, type 2 diabetes, high blood pressure, high cholesterol and bowel cancer. It is also a fuel for the bacteria in our gut, which will be explored later. We should eat a minimum of thirty grams of fibre a day, which would be the equivalent of a daily intake of a bowl of porridge, a banana, two slices of wholegrain toast, half a tin of baked beans, one portion of broccoli and an apple.

Although fat often gets a bad press, we need it as an energy source, it provides essential fatty acids required for our cell membranes and it is necessary to absorb certain vitamins. However, not all fats are created equally. They differ in their chemical composition and have different effects on our health. Omega-3 fatty acids – found in oily fish, walnuts, flax and chia seeds – are reported to have anti-inflammatory properties and may protect against heart disease and some cancers. But saturated and trans fats – typically solid at room temperature and found in animal products, tropical oils, industrially-produced baked products, and oils used for deep frying – are known to increase the amount of harmful cholesterol in our body. Olive oil is often recommended as a healthier alternative to butter or margarine – this is due to its chemical structure: it is high in monounsaturated fats, which are better for heart health. Rapeseed oil is another good alternative as it is high in the omega-3 fatty acid alpha-linolenic acid (ALA), as well as the antioxidant vitamin E. It also has a higher smoke point than olive oil so is suitable for cooking at higher temperatures.

Best balance

The best ratio of proteins, carbohydrates and fats that we should eat will vary between different people, but here is a guide:

Proteins: between 10 and 30 per cent of our calorie intake
Carbohydrates: between 45 and 65 per cent of our calorie intake
Fats: between 25 and 35 per cent of our calorie intake

A sample meal with approximately this ratio would be a wholemeal bagel filled with a chicken breast and avocado.

Micronutrients

Micronutrients are substances which are essential for life but only in tiny amounts. They include minerals, such as calcium and iron, and vitamins. Most of us can get almost all of the micronutrients we need through eating a diet rich in fruit, vegetables, nuts and cereals. However, some people, including women trying to conceive and those with specific deficiencies, will need certain supplements. In the UK it is advisable to consider a vitamin D supplement during the winter months, some people may need it throughout the entire year.

How to eat healthily

There are many different diet plans, which include different amounts of macronutrients and micronutrients. These include wholefood plant-based diets, low-carb high-fat, keto, Paleo, vegan, vegetarian and pescatarian. If you look hard enough into the scientific literature, it is possible to find studies that both support and refute the benefits of each of these. However, there are several general principles which can be applied to whatever plan you follow:

- **Maximise your fruit and vegetable intake**. In the UK, it is recommended that we eat at least five portions of fruit and vegetables every day, but less than a third of adults manage this, and even fewer children. If we ate even greater amounts, this is likely to be even better for our wellbeing. Fruit and vegetables are vital for our health. They are packed with fibre, along with a multitude of vitamins, minerals and antioxidants. There is evidence that diets high in plant-based products are associated with a reduced risk of heart disease, stroke, some types of cancer and obesity. Some easy ways to boost your intake include:

  - Add a handful of berries or a chopped banana to your morning cereal or porridge.
  - If you snack between meals, choose fruit or vegetables. Some fascinating research has shown that snacking on fruit is associated with lower levels of anxiety, depression and emotional distress than snacking on crisps or chocolate.
  - Make a conscious effort to include vegetables with every meal, and try and use them to fill at least half of your plate.
  - Smoothies and soups can be a great way of consuming several portions of fruit or vegetables, and they are also a good way

to 'use up' produce that might have started to go past its best.

- Keep fruit and vegetables somewhere where they can easily be seen (the impact of this will be explored in the chapter on Goal Setting and Habits).

- Aim to eat at least five portions of fruit or vegetables before you have any 'unhealthy' snacks. If you are tempted to eat cake, have an apple first, then reassess how you feel.

- Frozen products are often cheaper than fresh, and they have the additional advantage of lasting for longer.

- If you have children, encourage them to eat lots of fruit and vegetables from an early age, so that it becomes a habit and is seen as the 'normal' way of eating.

- **Eat the rainbow**. Fruits and vegetables come in an incredible array of colours. These colours are the result of phytochemicals, which are chemical compounds that act as natural pesticides to protect plants from predators such as insects. They may also have benefits for us humans too. For example, lycopene, which gives tomatoes their red colour, is thought to have antioxidant properties which may help in reducing our risk of developing heart disease. Beta-carotene gives an orange/yellow colour, as seen in carrots, and is converted to vitamin A in the body, where it plays a role in keeping our eyes healthy. Although the research into phytochemicals is largely in its infancy, it is recommended that we consume as many different-coloured fruits and vegetables as possible to maximise the diversity of phytochemicals and micronutrients we take on board.

- **Increase your fibre consumption**. Most of us don't get enough fibre in our diets. Some of the best sources of fibre include fruit and vegetables, oats, beans and wholegrain products such as wholegrain rice. When we start to increase our fibre consumption, it's a good plan to do it gradually and to make sure we drink enough water. We will initially produce more gas, which can sometimes be uncomfortable, and we need to make sure that we have enough fluid on board to 'keep things moving'. Simple ways to increase our fibre intake are to swap 'white' foods for their wholegrain equivalents, for example, bread and pasta, and to focus on eating lots of plant-based foods.

- **Reduce your intake of ultra-processed foods**. Processed foods are foods that have been altered or changed in some way as part of their preparation, for example, through canning, pickling or drying. Many foods have been processed in some way and not all processing is unhealthy, for example, one study reported that frozen fruit and vegetables may have a higher nutrient content than their fresh counterparts. However, many ultra-processed foods have sugars, salt, fat, sweeteners or preservatives added to improve their taste and prolong their shelf life. Generally, ultra-processed foods are not healthy. They are associated with a higher energy intake and weight gain, as we tend to overeat processed products, and some can disrupt our gut bacteria. If we're filling up on processed products, we are less likely to be consuming the healthy food sources that we actually need.

  The best approach is to focus our diet on wholefoods in their natural state and to try and cook from scratch. This doesn't need to be time consuming or complicated – a simple and nutritious bolognese can be prepared quickly using just onion, mushrooms, carrots, red lentils and tomatoes.

- **Reduce your added sugar intake**. The World Health Organisation (WHO) advises that less than ten per cent of our daily energy intake should come from free sugars, which are sugars added to foods and drinks, along with the sugars present in honey, syrups, fruit juices and juice concentrates. It would be even better if we could reduce this amount to five per cent, which is around five teaspoons. A high-sugar intake is associated with dental disease, being overweight or obese, high blood pressure and high serum lipids. When we eat sugar, it triggers the release of the 'feel-good' chemical, dopamine, in our brain. This can result in cravings for sweet foods as we are seeking that pleasurable sensation. When we reduce our intake of free sugars, our cravings subside over time. Strategies to reduce our sugar consumption include the obvious choices, such as swapping biscuits and cakes for fruit and vegetables and drinking water instead of fizzy drinks. However, sugars are added to many other products, which we might not realise, such as yoghurts, tomato ketchup and salad cream. It's generally helpful to choose foods which are as close to their natural state as possible, for example, natural yoghurt instead of flavoured yoghurts.

- **Be mindful of your fat consumption**. In recent years there has been some debate as to the role that fats have in causing disease. Traditionally, we were advised to have a low-fat diet if we wanted to reduce the risk of heart disease. However, we are now aware that certain fats, such as omega-3 fatty acids, can be beneficial for our health, and these are now recommended as part of a healthy diet. The WHO suggests that less than thirty per cent of our energy intake overall should come from fats and that unsaturated fats are better than saturated fats, as the latter can raise our cholesterol levels. Saturated fats, which are usually found in animal-derived products, should account for no more than ten per cent of our energy intake. In real terms, this is equivalent to around three tablespoons of butter or a big slice of cheese (around one hundred grams).

The types of foods that contain 'healthy fats', and which we should aim to include in our diets, include oily fish, avocado, nuts and olive oil.

To avoid harmful fats, we can boil or steam food instead of frying it, we can choose lean cuts of meat and we can avoid manufactured goods such as doughnuts, which may contain high levels of trans fats.

- **Salt**. Most of us consume too much salt in our diets. Even if we don't add it to our food, it is a hidden ingredient in many processed foods and increases our risk of developing high blood pressure, and therefore heart disease and stroke. We should be eating no more than five grams a day. This is approximately equivalent to a bowl of cornflakes, a packet of crisps and a bacon sandwich. The best way to avoid excess salt is to minimise our intake of processed foods and to be aware that many food products may have added salt in them, for example, processed meats, ready-made cooking sauces and tinned soup.

- **Water**. Water is another essential component of a healthy diet. If we are mildly dehydrated, this can have a negative impact on our mood, concentration span and energy levels. The exact amount we need depends on different factors such as how active we are and the climate, but most adults need around one and a half litres a day. Many people choose drinks which are full of sugar, caffeine, alcohol or artificial ingredients to quench their thirst, but water really is the healthiest option.

- **Moderate your alcohol consumption**. A lot of us may have first-hand experience of the effects of drinking alcohol. In the short term, when we have an alcoholic drink it can help us to feel relaxed, happy and confident, but when large amounts are consumed, this can result in poor judgement, loss of control, slurred speech, poor balance, vomiting, incontinence and even coma and death. Although alcohol is a sedative and helps us to fall asleep quickly, it impairs the quality of sleep. Alcohol results in less rapid eye movement (REM) or 'restorative' sleep, meaning that we feel tired the day after drinking. This can adversely impact our health-related behaviours, as we may be less likely to exercise and more likely to eat unhealthy foods if we are fatigued or 'hungover'.

Alcohol itself is highly calorific – a pint of beer contains around the same number of calories as a Mars bar. These calories are often described as 'empty calories' as they don't have any nutritional value.

In the long term, excessive use of alcohol increases the risk of many diseases including heart disease, stroke, liver disease, head and neck cancers, oesophageal cancer, liver cancer, breast cancer and bowel cancer. It also impacts the composition of the bacteria that live in our guts and can exacerbate the symptoms of mental health diseases, such as depression.

The current UK recommendations are that adults should drink a maximum of fourteen units of alcohol a week, this should be spread over at least three days and you should aim to have several alcohol-free days every week. The number of units of alcohol in a drink varies depending upon its strength and volume, but as a rough guide, there is one unit in a single shot of spirit, there are two units in a standard glass of wine and there are three units in a pint of strong beer.

Despite these recommendations, several studies have reported that there is no safe level of alcohol intake when it comes to brain health or cancer risk.

The role of fasting

Intermittent fasting (IF) has become incredibly popular in the fields of health and wellness over the past decade, but it isn't a new trend. Fasting is deeply embedded in many religious practices, and ancient physicians such as Hippocrates believed it was a useful tool in allowing the body to heal from certain illnesses.

The term 'intermittent fasting' is used by different people to mean different things – some individuals fast on alternate days whilst others follow an eating pattern such as 5:2, during which they eat normally on five days of the week but eat a limited number of calories on the remaining two days. Strictly speaking, intermittent fasting involves a period during which we don't eat or drink anything that contains any energy or which can cause a rise in our insulin levels. It has also been described as 'time-restricted feeding' or 'time-restricted eating'. During the fasting hours, the only drinks that are allowed are water, black coffee, black tea and green tea. Some of the most popular ways of doing this are 14:10 or 16:8, during which we only eat during a ten- or eight-hour window over each twenty-four-hour period.

So, what is the point of IF? IF has been shown to have several benefits for health. When we eat and our blood sugar levels rise, our bodies release insulin. Insulin allows muscle, liver and fat cells to take up this sugar. When the energy we take in is greater than the energy we are burning, excess energy is stored as fat. In the 'fed' state, insulin levels are high, whereas in the 'fasting' state, insulin levels fall, and stored sugar forms can be mobilised for energy. One of the benefits of IF is that if we fast for long enough periods, this allows the body to use fat as fuel, which is one of the reasons why IF can be helpful for weight loss. Also, we are likely to eat less food if our eating window has been shortened.

However, the benefits of IF aren't just limited to losing weight. Studies have shown that when we switch to the fasted state, this turns on a variety of pathways which help to improve our metabolism, reduce inflammation, enhance brain function, potentially reduce the risk of some cancers, improve blood sugar control, improve blood pressure and slow the effects of ageing.

Is intermittent fasting for me?

Intermittent fasting has many recognised health benefits, but it isn't for everyone. There are certain people whom IF wouldn't necessarily be suitable for, including pregnant women, those with a history of eating disorders and those who need to take medication with meals at certain times of the day. I know many friends and colleagues who do intermittent fasting and feel much better for it, but for me personally, it's not something I practise. I have tried it several times and have given sufficient time for my body to adapt, but I found that I was constantly thinking about food (even when I wasn't hungry!) and it took some of the joy out of my life and eating. I love my morning coffee to have frothy milk in it and I enjoy my exercise a lot more when I am properly fuelled. Although I don't fast for prolonged periods, I do try to eat in a 'circadian pattern' so that I eat during daylight hours, usually from 7 am to 6 pm, and I don't snack in the evenings. There is evidence that fasts of thirteen hours may have health benefits, for example, in reducing the risk of certain cancers. As with all healthy choices, it's important that you find those that you enjoy and those that are sustainable.

If you do decide to give IF a go, it can be helpful to start with a longer eating window to allow your body to get used to it, for example, ten hours. You could then reduce the duration once you've adapted. For example, you might begin eating between 10 am and 8 pm, then after a few weeks modify this to midday to 8 pm.

Anjalee, doctor, age 38

I love to eat, and I also love to cook. I admit, I am a feeder, and food is my love language. I aspire to be one of those cuddly grandmas who loves to feed anyone coming into her home.

Cooking wasn't something that came naturally to me. I was raised in a Gujarati household. Our staple diet, prepared by my mum, was homemade chapatis. These are thin flatbreads made with finely milled wholewheat flour, toasted on a pan and then covered in a thin layer of butter. We would eat these accompanied by white rice and either a vegetable curry or a mixed lentil dhal. My mum would also have a ready-available stash of homemade live-cultured yoghurt – as children, we ate this to help reduce the spiciness of the chilli in the curry! I didn't really enjoy these meals – I would often only manage to nibble through half a chapati, and I would then snack for the rest of the day. I was more interested in studying and watching TV than learning how to cook or about healthy nutrition. I would crave westernised meals such as pizza, pasta or sausage and mash. When I went to university and lived away from my parents, I usually ate quick and easy foods, such as instant noodles.

It wasn't until I got married and had children that I started to take an interest in healthy eating. I didn't know how to prepare chapatis, so I started by making wholesome dhals. I realised that they were packed full of 'superfoods' such as turmeric, ginger, various pulses, and many other ingredients which can help digestion, gut health and immunity. As my knowledge and confidence grew, I began to branch out with the variety of dishes I made, and I spent time finding healthier ways to prepare traditional Gujarati foods.

I now focus on eating healthily daily, and we enjoy home-cooked easy-to-make meals. I try to keep things as simple but as tasty as possible to fit into a busy lifestyle and around young children. I have found delicious, nutritious small changes that have been really beneficial. For example, to reduce our intake of unhealthy fats, I have replaced the butters and oils in our food with avocados, nuts and seeds where possible. Treats for my children are often fruit-focused – they love watermelon, so I will often cut up watermelon into sticks, which I freeze to make lollies. We enjoy variety in our diet, so I dabble with foods from around the world to keep things interesting.

One of the healthiest changes my husband and I have made has been to reduce our alcohol intake. We were never heavy drinkers, but during the pandemic, we wanted to mark weekends. We started 'Margarita Fridays', ending the week with a cocktail. However, once the restrictions came to an end, our Fridays did not. We still had our weekly cocktails, but we would also socialise with friends and family, and almost every meal would include alcohol. Before long, our weight had increased and we were feeling sluggish. We decided to stop drinking other than on special occasions, and this one change has made a huge difference to our mood, wellbeing, weight and finances.

I also practise intermittent fasting, so I eat my meals between a window of 12–8 pm. This helps me to focus on what I put into my body and has stopped me snacking at night-time once my children are asleep. The lack of snacking has also meant my sleep has improved. I feel much brighter for it, I have a lot more mental clarity during the day and I am more productive, energised and happier.

The importance of maintaining a healthy weight

Obesity is a major health concern worldwide, affecting one in four adults in the UK. It can reduce our life expectancy by up to ten years and contributes to at least one in every thirteen deaths in Europe. Obesity increases the risk of many diseases, including type 2 diabetes, heart disease, asthma, bowel cancer, breast cancer, gallstones and arthritis. Very importantly, being overweight can reduce our quality of life, and can be associated with low self-esteem, low levels of confidence, tiredness and back pain.

Our weight is the result of a complex interaction between many different factors, for example, our appetite, certain hormones, our gut bacteria and our muscle mass. In simple terms, our weight results from the energy we take in from what we eat and drink, and the energy we use. At any given point in time, it is thought that at least one in every three adults are trying to lose weight, which isn't easy for many people. Here are some general lifestyle changes that you can make if you're trying to lose weight:

- Be **NEAT**! NEAT stands for non-exercise activity thermogenesis and describes the energy we burn doing anything that isn't sleeping, eating or formal sport-like exercise. It includes activities such as walking to work, washing the dishes and fidgeting. If we're trying to lose weight, it is helpful to increase our NEAT score. This simply means keep moving whenever you can. Even chores like ironing and hanging out the washing are beneficial.
- **Exercise**. Exercise has many benefits for our health and wellbeing, one of which is that it uses energy, so is an important tool in weight loss.
- Be **SMART**. Set goals which are SMART. This means that they are Specific, Measurable, Achievable, Realistic and Time-bound. So, rather than say: 'I want to lose weight by my birthday', it is much more effective to say: 'I want to lose five kilograms in five weeks. I will have achieved my target weight by 22nd February.' This give us specific targets to work towards and, by doing this, we can monitor our progress more effectively. Goals will be explored later in this book.
- **Monitor your weight** at regular intervals, for example, weekly. This can help to show you what you are achieving, which can be highly motivational.
- **Be patient**. It's really easy to become disheartened if we're not losing weight as quickly as we'd like. Some weeks we may even put on a few pounds. The important thing is that we see the big picture — the best way to lose weight safely and effectively is to aim for slow and sustainable weight loss. There isn't a 'quick fix'. Achieving and maintaining a healthy weight needs continued effort over time, along with continued

tweaks to our diet and activity levels. Ideally, the maximum amount of weight we should aim to lose is one kilogram a week.

- **Watch what you drink**. Alcohol, fruit juice and many fizzy drinks contain lots of calories. You could swap these for water – this change doesn't take much effort but can have a big impact.
- **Eat slowly**. There is evidence to suggest that eating slowly can reduce the amount you eat during a meal and can reduce feelings of hunger. It can be helpful to eat mindfully, focusing on how your meal looks, smells and tastes. Some people like to make a conscious effort to chew for longer.
- **Pay attention to your hunger signals**. Sometimes we carry on eating, even though we know we are full. Take note of the messages your body is sending you. There is a Japanese phrase, *Hara hachi bu*, which means 'eat until you are eighty per cent full'. The phrase originated from the city of Okinawa, and it is an eating philosophy which many Japanese people live by. The people from Okinawa have one of the longest life expectancies around the world, which goes hand in hand with low rates of chronic diseases.
- **Eat at a table**. Many people have hectic lives, and mealtimes are 'squeezed in' here and there, rather than being a main event, for example, we may eat lunch sat at our desk or have our dinner in front of the television. Studies have shown that we are more likely to eat more when we're not paying attention to our plate, so eating at a table can help to reduce this effect. It can have additional benefits as well – if we're eating with other people, it can strengthen social ties, and if we're having a break from work it can help to restore our mental energy levels.
- **Be aware of your portion sizes**. I know many people who find it hard to lose weight even though their diet seems to be healthy. Sometimes this is because they have got used to eating large portions of food! Ways to reduce portion size

include using a smaller plate, filling half of the plate with vegetables or salad so there is less room for the higher energy components of the meal and, once a meal has been served, immediately put away any leftover food so there is not the temptation to go back for a second helping.

- **Use an app to track calories**. It can be very hard to know exactly how much energy is in the foods that we eat. There are many free apps that will calculate this. When people start to log their calories, they're often surprised at how much they really consume.

- **Be proud of your body**. If we're trying to lose weight, it can be easy to focus on what we'd like to change with our bodies, rather than realise how awesome they already are. This can have a negative impact on our self-esteem. It is helpful to appreciate that, although we're working towards a healthy weight to improve our health and wellbeing, our bodies are incredible, and our weight doesn't define us. List five things that your body can already achieve, for example, it can carry heavy bags of shopping, it can walk the children to school, it allows you to cycle to work, it gives warm hugs and it can dance in a kitchen disco.

- **Eat balanced meals**. Aim to fill half of your plate (or bowl) with fruit and vegetables, one quarter with complex carbohydrates in the form of whole grains or starchy vegetables, and one quarter with lean protein. Add in a source of healthy fat, and you've got yourself a satisfying, balanced meal. Fibre from complex carbohydrates is low in energy density and helps us feel fuller, which can help with weight maintenance. Similarly, protein has a satiating effect and can be beneficial for appetite control.

Dr Aishah Iqbal, medical doctor and weight loss coach
When your best friend is in the middle of a competition or is working towards a promotion at work, your role is to cheer. You give words of support and highlight the successes they have

previously achieved. You do this to help your friend to move forward on their journey and to keep them motivated to get to the finish line. Pointing out flaws or choosing negative words wouldn't work. It could damage confidence, reduce drive and initiate a negative pathway of 'I'm no good, I can't do this, I'll give up'.

When it comes to losing weight, you must be your own cheerleader. Many people who are trying to lose weight find themselves using negative phrases to describe themselves and their body, for example, it is common to hear people saying, 'I'm fat' or 'I'm lazy'. This can reduce motivation, can trigger unhealthy behaviours and can cause self-loathing, which is detrimental to feeling physically and mentally fit and strong.

Being overweight results from a multitude of complex factors, including genetics, hormones, the gut microbiota, finances, level of education and the environment. Whilst several of these might not be directly in your control, you can focus on those that are, including your mindset.

The thoughts you think and the words you speak are your own creation. This means that if you find yourself caught in negative thoughts, you have the power to pull yourself out and to change your patterns of thinking. To do this, you first need to recognise what is happening in your mind. You may find that a thought triggers an emotion that may then cause you to behave in a certain way. For example, if you think you're lazy, this could cause you to feel angry towards yourself, which might result in you eating a bar of chocolate. Once you have identified that you are thinking or saying something that goes against the outcome you are looking for, stop yourself and ask, 'how can I reframe my thoughts in a more positive way?'. It can be helpful to highlight what you have achieved – consider what positive things your body has done that day. You might have carried the shopping to the car, done some gardening or walked the children to school. Recognise and celebrate your achievements, no matter how small they are.

It takes time and practice to become aware of negative thoughts and to replace them with positive or kind ones. However, it is absolutely worth it as it helps us to view ourselves with compassion and increases our motivation to take actions that move us towards our goals.

The gut microbiome

There has been an explosion of interest in the gut microbiome over the last decade, particularly in the role it plays in health and disease. The gut microbiome describes the trillions of microorganisms which live in our intestines, specifically it describes their genetic material. This largely consists of bacteria but also includes viruses, protozoa, fungi and other classes of microorganisms. These microorganisms can weigh up to a whopping two kilograms! Interestingly, we have more bacterial DNA inside us than we do our own DNA: for every one human gene we have, we have over a hundred bacterial genes.

What does the microbiome do?

If we think of our bodies as hotels, the bacteria that live inside us are not merely the guests of the hotel. Quite the opposite in fact. They are part of the workforce – the cleaners, security team and chefs – who work tirelessly behind the scenes to help keep everything running smoothly.

Our gut bacteria have many important roles. They are involved in harvesting energy from the food we eat, the functioning of our immune system, the production of chemical messengers such as serotonin and the production of vitamins such as vitamin K. One of the major functions of the microbiome is to ferment non-digestible dietary fibre. This produces short-chain fatty acids (SCFAs), which are involved in weight control, sensitivity to insulin, reduction of inflammation and preventing bowel cancer. SCFAs can modulate our appetite, the amount of energy we extract from food and how our food is used in our bodies.

Our gut is also intimately associated with our brain and how it functions. It has long been known the gut and the brain can communicate with each other. Most of us have experienced the sensation of 'butterflies in our stomach' if we feel nervous, and we may suffer from diarrhoea or nausea if we are stressed. This communication occurs through neural, hormonal, immune and metabolic pathways. The gut microbiome has an important role to play in this. For example, the bacteria which reside in our intestines can affect the activity in our nerves, immune system and hormonal systems and it is through these pathways that the gut microbiome may have an impact on mental health disorders such as stress, anxiety and depression.

What influences the composition of our microbiome?

Although inherited factors play a small part in determining the composition of our gut microbiome, environmental factors are much more significant. These include the mode of our delivery (vaginal birth or caesarean section), whether we were breast-fed or formula-fed, the medications we have taken (especially antibiotics), how much exercise we get, our sleeping patterns and our stress levels. However, the most important factor is our diet, in particular, our fibre intake and the diversity of plant-based products that we consume. To increase the numbers and diversity of bacteria in our intestines, it is really important to eat a diet rich in fruit, vegetables and other sources of fibre.

To further boost our microbiome, it is also helpful to reduce our intake of sugar, saturated fats and to avoid excessive protein consumption (although some protein is vital for health). There is some evidence that artificial sweeteners might disrupt the balance of our microbiome, along with food additives such as emulsifiers, which are very common in processed foods. If we aim to improve our eating habits and boost our fibre intake, we can see improvements in the composition of our gut bacteria within a matter of days.

The microbiome in disease

It is believed that a high diversity of gut bacteria is needed for good health. A reduction in diversity is associated with a range of diseases including inflammatory bowel disease, diabetes, obesity and arthritis. But it is important to remember that it's not always certain whether the imbalance is a cause or effect of the disease in question.

For some diseases, there is evidence that the gut microbiome has a causative role. For example, overweight and obese individuals generally have lower bacterial diversity than healthy people, and studies in mice have shown that mice who receive bacteria from obese individuals gain more weight than mice who receive microorganisms from healthy people.

What about prebiotics and probiotics?

There's often a lot of talk in the media about prebiotics and probiotics, but what exactly are they? **Prebiotics** are the fuels used by the bacteria in our gut. Some of the foods with the best reputation as prebiotics include asparagus, Jerusalem artichoke, garlic, onions and leek. It's great if you can aim to include these on your plate. **Probiotics** describe the actual live bacteria themselves. The formal definition of probiotics according to the World Health Organisation is 'live microorganisms which when administered in adequate amounts confer a health benefit on the host'. Probiotics, particularly species such as *Bifidobacterium* and *Lactobacillus*, have been included in a wide range of food products and supplements, including yoghurts and drinks, and they may be found in fermented foods such as sauerkraut and kefir. It's useful to know that different 'probiotic products' contain different amounts of bacteria and different species and strains of bacteria. In some cases, live bacteria may not actually reach the gut, so may not have any effects, as they can be destroyed by stomach acid and digestive enzymes. However, there is evidence that with some formulations, ingested bacteria do reach the intestines, where they can positively influence our microbiome. The probiotic bacteria don't take up permanent residence, meaning that they won't actually 'move in' and live there, but they can boost our healthy bacteria, for example, by providing energy sources that promote their growth.

Although probiotics are generally safe, they should be avoided by certain people, including those who are immunocompromised.

To sum up, our gut microbiome describes the trillions of microorganisms that live in our intestines. These microbes have a range of different jobs including helping with digestion, metabolism, mental health and our immune system. For good health, you should try to maximise the range of bacteria in the gut. To do this, eat a diet rich in fibre and reduce your intake of sugar and processed foods.

How to implement healthy eating patterns

What I often find is that although people have the knowledge about how to eat healthily, they don't put that knowledge into action. Most people know that it's better to eat an apple rather than a chocolate bar, but the chocolate often wins! There are several reasons for this. Our eating habits are often deeply ingrained from an early age, and we tend to do what we have always done. Many of the foods that we should be cutting down on contain high levels of sugar. As mentioned previously, sugar triggers the release of dopamine, which plays an important role in the reward pathways in our brain. It's not easy to stop doing something that gives us pleasure. Sacrificing an immediate joy for a long-term health gain can be difficult. It's made even harder by the fact that we're bombarded by clever advertising and marketing campaigns. In addition to this, sugar-rich foods result in a spike in our blood sugar levels and are described as having a high glycaemic index. This can be unhelpful – as our blood sugar levels fall, we can start to feel hungry again, which can cause us to eat when we may not actually need to.

Whilst many healthy behaviours give us an immediate boost, for example, that post-run high or the feeling of being refreshed after a good night's sleep, we don't necessarily get the same hit from eating a wholegrain slice of toast.

In essence, adopting healthy eating patterns can require us to cut down on the things we enjoy, without us seeing immediate benefit.

So, what can we do about this? I admit it's not always easy. However, once we have made healthy eating a habit, we will do it routinely, and we feel so much better for it. Establishing habits is explored later in this book, but some of my top tips relating specifically to nutrition are:

- **Make small changes**. When we first embark upon our nutrition journey it can be tempting to try and overhaul our eating patterns completely and make huge changes from the outset. Whilst this strategy can work for some people, for many it is overwhelming. It is often more sensible to start with small changes, and when those changes become our new normal, we can add something else. For example, we can start by focusing on just one meal a day. Think about the ways you could include fruit for breakfast or try swapping your sugar-laden cereal for porridge or wholemeal toast. Once you've cracked breakfast, move on to lunch or dinner.
- **Start by adding rather than taking away**. Another action that a lot of people take when trying to improve their diet is to focus on what they have to give up, for example, crisps, rather than what they could add. It can be beneficial if our mental energy is spent on planning what extra foods we could add to our meals to make them healthier. Consider including broccoli alongside your lasagne or adding extra beans to your chilli. People often find that when they start to eat more plant-based foods and fibre, their tastes change and their desire for unhealthy foods starts to fade. Another strategy is to focus on

eating sufficient healthy foods before considering anything unhealthy, for example, only eating a cupcake once you have eaten at least five portions of fruit and vegetables. You may be surprised that you don't want the 'treat' at the end of it!

- **Try and make your environment as healthy as possible**. If you know you have a tendency to snack on crisps, remove that temptation and don't have them in your house. If we make our homes and workplaces as healthy as possible, for example, by having lots of easily accessible fruit and hiding away the cakes, this will make desirable behaviours much more likely.

- **Make healthy choices the easy choice**. As humans, we tend to carry out actions that are the easiest for us. You might have noticed that you would choose a banana from the fruit bowl rather than a melon. The reason for this is likely that it's easier for you to eat the banana. You can simply peel it rather than have to find a chopping board and knife. It's really helpful if you can apply the same principles to eating and cooking in general – have quick and easy foods readily available, for example, nuts to snack on or a pre-prepared meal ready for dinner.

- **Plan in advance** and think about what you will eat at mealtimes. If you have already decided to cook vegetable soup and have all the ingredients ready, you're much less likely to pop some chips in the oven for convenience. Batch cooking meals and freezing them is a good technique which can help with this.

- **Don't deprive yourself**. Sometimes we can eat healthily all day or all week, then 'overindulge' in treats in the evening or at weekends. There are several reasons for this, one being that we are simply hungry. It's important to make sure that we're sufficiently nourishing our bodies and that we don't feel deprived, as this increases the likelihood that we will eat more of the foods that give us an emotional boost.

- **Identify why you are eating**. There are many factors that cause us to eat – for example, we may be tired, or we may feel that we deserve a treat after a stressful day. Before opening the packet of biscuits, spend a moment to reflect upon why you want to eat. You might realise that you're eating for a reason that isn't hunger, and that then gives you the power to explore healthier ways to manage it.

- **Find the healthy foods that bring you joy**. We all need treats at times. Although Western society has frequently come to find its pleasure in highly processed and high-sugar products, there are many healthy alternatives that bring just as much, if not more, joy. My personal favourites are Medjool dates, pomegranate seeds, cashew nuts and raspberries.
- **Don't feel guilty**. If you overindulge, try not to feel guilty about it. It happens to us all! Just get back on the healthy wagon as soon as you can. It can take a while to change our eating patterns, as they are often deeply embedded habits. If we become aware that we are slipping back into unhealthy ways of eating, try and address this as soon as possible. A lot of unhealthy foods give us that dopamine hit, so we can rapidly become 'addicted' to them again.
- **See your changes as a positive lifestyle choice**. When we change our eating patterns, try to view this not as a diet but rather a lifestyle choice. You will feel great and are making a positive move to invest in your future.

Nourishing your body with a healthy diet will have a huge and positive impact on your physical and mental health and wellbeing. We all need carbohydrates, protein and fats along with an array of vitamins and minerals. Try to include lots of fruit, vegetables and fibre in your meals and minimise your intake of processed foods, sugar, salt and unhealthy fats. Ultimately, the best diet for you is one that you enjoy and which you can stick to in the long term.

Claire Hunter, Nutritional Therapy Practitioner

I think it's fair to say that, as a society, we have overcomplicated nutrition.

Diet culture promotes counting calories and macros and has got us labelling foods as 'good' and 'bad'.

The Health at Every Size movement says we should stop worrying about our body weight and tells us that we can be healthy regardless of the number on the scale.

Reductionists encourage us to take supplements of individual micronutrients, fill our shopping trolleys with superfoods, shun carbs, or eat more protein than is necessary.

Advocates of fad diets want us to believe their chosen eating pattern is going to help us lose weight more effectively than any other diet we've tried before.

The media does a fantastic job of grabbing our attention with sensationalist headlines that are designed to generate clicks, but many articles don't give a balanced overview of the evidence. As a result, this often unfairly discredits public health messages around nutrition.

Self-proclaimed celebrity 'nutrition experts' bombard us with messaging on their huge public platforms, hooking us in with their 'revelatory' claims that their protocol is going to cure us of our ailments. All we have to do is buy their book, supplement, or online course and we'll be healed!

And we live in an obesogenic environment where everywhere we turn, we are encouraged to eat. And not just to eat, but to consume foods that are highly palatable with excessive amounts of additives that we ought to be more aware of, and which drive our energy intake beyond our expenditure, leading to weight gain.

With all these distractions, it's not surprising that we seem to have lost sight of the bigger picture where nutrition science is concerned.

Nutrition is nuanced. There's often no black-and-white answer. At a basic level, your gender, age and health status will dictate the answer to the question 'what should I eat?'. Then there's the matter of context. Are fried eggs healthy? Compared to what? A deep-fried mars bar or a three-bean salad?

The thing is, universal evidence-based nutrition advice is fairly boring, and it's nothing groundbreaking. It's not very exciting to tell people to eat more fruit, vegetables, and fibre, drink more water, and watch their intake of saturated fat, added sugars and salt.

But, in many cases, it really is as simple as that.

If we look at populations where people live longest with the lowest incidences of disability due to chronic lifestyle diseases, we see a pattern. In these so-called Blue Zones, diets are comprised of whole foods, predominantly of plant origin.

Although these Blue Zones can be found around the world – in Costa Rica, Italy, Greece, Japan and even America – their eating pattern is similar to what you may be familiar with as a traditional Mediterranean diet. This doesn't mean they eat nothing but pasta swimming in olive oil, washed down with red wine. Nor are they vegans or vegetarians. They simply prioritise whole grains, beans, lentils, seasonal fruit and vegetables (especially leafy greens), nuts and seeds. Meat, poultry, fish, eggs and dairy products are consumed in varying quantities, but meat, when eaten, is typically viewed as a celebration food.

Worldwide, public health recommendations are largely similar. The UK's Eatwell Guide; the MyPlate dietary guidelines in America, Canada's Food Guide, and the Australian Guide to Healthy Eating all share the same common message; plant foods should be the foundation of your meals, complemented by lean protein and low-fat dairy (or plant-based alternatives).

There's really no need to overcomplicate the way we eat for optimal health.

If we all ate according to these guidelines, our risk of developing lifestyle diseases like type 2 diabetes, cardiovascular disease, stroke and even some cancers would be greatly reduced, and lives would be saved as a result. We wouldn't need to worry about calories, macro ratios, or whether we can be metabolically healthy with a high BMI. Individual macronutrients and micronutrients wouldn't be a concern because we'd be getting everything we needed from a balanced diet. Fad diets would be a thing of the past and we could all happily ignore media propaganda.

I might die waiting for this to happen, but in the meantime, take most of what you read about nutrition with a pinch of (iodised low sodium) salt; if it sounds too good to be true, it probably is!

My personal story, Claire Hunter
I don't need convincing about the power of the gut microbiota.

For around the last fifteen years, I've had irritable bowel syndrome (IBS). It started after a particularly bad bout of gastroenteritis, and it basically felt like the gastroenteritis never went away.

But looking back, there were a few clues that this could happen.

As a child and young adult, I was sicklier than most. I'd estimate that as a result of recurrent tonsillitis, infected wisdom teeth, several operations (including an appendicectomy) and meningococcal septicaemia, I've taken around fifty courses of antibiotics in my lifetime. Some of these were lifesaving and one hundred per cent necessary. Others I'm not so sure about.

I believe that these inadvertent assaults on my gut microbiota created the perfect storm for my chronic digestive condition. While we don't know exactly what causes IBS, it's thought to be multifactorial, and something that may be involved is the gut microbiota, whose composition is altered by antibiotics.

Throughout my life, I probably ate a healthier diet than most people, although my meals had revolved around meat and other animal products. I got my five-a-day, but I was brought up on 'meat and two veg'. But during my nutrition training, there was one dietary pattern that kept cropping up in discussions as potentially being the most beneficial for health.

Want to improve your chances of conceiving? The Mediterranean diet looks promising. Got type 2 diabetes? Eat a high-fibre, low-GI (glycaemic index) diet to control your blood sugar levels. Wait, that's basically a Mediterranean diet. Concerned about cognitive decline and dementia? A Mediterranean-style diet appears to have protective effects. If you don't want to put a label on it, the takeaway information is that placing an emphasis on whole, unprocessed plant foods and reducing your consumption of red meat seems to support positive health outcomes.

Motivated by this information from an overall health perspective, slowly, I started eating more plants. First, I made my breakfasts entirely plant-based. Then lunch. Then I had two meat-free dinners a week until, gradually, I had transitioned to a diet that is at least ninety-five per cent plants. I now make beans, lentils and soy products like tofu and tempeh, the centrepiece of my meals, and I try to focus on plant diversity, so I am nourishing my gut microbiota with a variety of prebiotic fibre, probiotic-rich fermented foods and polyphenol phytochemicals.

The effect this had on my IBS was powerful. My symptoms dramatically reduced and for the first time since I could remember, I felt like I had a fully functioning digestive system.

I look forward to seeing how this exciting and rapidly evolving area of research develops, and how in future we might understand more about the role of the gut microbes in disease prediction, disease prevention and disease management.

Environment: How do the Natural Environment and Digital Environment affect our Wellbeing?

Dr Emma Short

Our environment describes everything that surrounds us – the country we live in, our town, our home and workplace, even the weather. It has long been known that our environment affects our health. People who have high levels of sun exposure have an increased risk of developing skin cancer, air pollution can exacerbate lung diseases and poor water quality is associated with gastrointestinal disease.

Over the twentieth and twenty-first centuries, there has been a huge change in how people spend their time. Instead of being outside in the natural environment working, playing, walking or socialising, we are increasingly glued to our screens. When computers were first invented, they were very much a tool that was in our control and they were used for basic functions such as calculations and writing documents. With the digital revolution, we have become reliant on our digital devices, which now have a major role in the workplace, education, communications and our relationships.

I'm hoping that this chapter will remind you of the magic of nature and will encourage you to spend more time in green areas. I will also look at how screen time and social media affect our wellbeing and consider the ways we can use technology safely.

The healing power of nature

Being outside is good for us. We've all experienced feeling calmer or rejuvenated after a forest walk or a day at the beach. Unfortunately, in recent years, we've become increasingly disconnected from the natural environment. We've got so caught up in 'doing' that we're neglecting simply 'being'. Modern life is stressful, and around one in every four of us will experience mental health difficulties each year.

A wealth of scientific research has proven that spending time in nature is beneficial for our health, especially for our mental wellbeing, our cardiovascular system and our immune system. This knowledge has prompted policymakers around the world to try to improve access to green areas as a priority for improving human health. A 2020 Public Health England Report stated that: 'There is increasingly compelling evidence showing that access to green spaces really matters for our health ... there is much we can and must do.' The report highlighted 'new evidence and actions to help local areas consider how good quality greenspace can support the delivery of health, social, environmental and economic priorities, at a relatively low cost'.

Shinrin-Yoku

Much of the research surrounding the healing power of nature has explored Shinrin-Yoku, or forest bathing, which involves immersing yourself in greenery rather than water. The term 'Shinrin-Yoku' was first used by the Director of the Japanese Forestry Agency in 1982. It describes being in a forest and using all your senses to engage with the natural environment. Although forest bathing usually involves a slow walk, the aim of the practice isn't to exercise. Rather it's a restorative, gentle, mindful experience.

Shinrin-Yoku and mental health

Being in nature has a powerful effect on our mental wellbeing. Studies have shown that spending time surrounded by trees reduces the symptoms of depression and anxiety and can improve our mood. It reduces anger and helps us to feel less fatigued. Forest bathing also reduces our stress levels and calms us. Many studies that have examined the effects of forest bathing on our mental state have used questionnaires to explore mental wellbeing, but several studies have also measured salivary and/or urinary levels of stress hormones such as cortisol and adrenaline. These have shown that the subjective improvement in stress levels is accompanied by a physiological improvement as well, with a measurable reduction in the levels of our stress hormones.

When we practise Shinrin-Yoku, we experience an increase in alpha and beta brainwaves. This is associated with feelings of relaxation, alertness and enhanced learning. Forest bathing may even play a role in improving our self-esteem, our attention span and our cognitive functioning.

Shinrin-Yoku and our cardiovascular system

Our cardiovascular system describes our heart and blood vessels. Heart disease is the biggest killer in the developed world. The traditional risk factors for heart disease are high blood pressure, high cholesterol levels, smoking, a family history of heart disease and diabetes. We know that many of these can be modified through our lifestyle and our behaviours. Spending time in nature has beneficial effects on our cardiovascular system.

Research has shown that forest environments can reduce our systolic and diastolic blood pressure (the top and bottom numbers of our blood pressure readings) and they can reduce our heart rate. These effects are seen because forest bathing increases the activity of our parasympathetic or 'rest and restore' nervous system and reduces activity in our sympathetic or 'stress' nervous system.

Shinrin-Yoku and our immune system

Our immune system helps to protect us from microorganisms which could cause disease, such as bacteria, viruses and fungi. It also has a role in protecting against cancer. Our immune system includes white blood cells, some of which are called Natural Killer cells, or NK cells. These cells are important in fighting viruses and in destroying cancer cells.

Spending time in nature boosts our numbers of NK cells and increases their activity levels, which may have antiviral effects. It also triggers the production of anti-cancer proteins and can modulate cytokine levels. Cytokines are small proteins which are especially important in helping cells to communicate with each other in immunity and inflammation. Forest bathing reduces the cytokines which promote inflammation. These effects are thought to be partially mediated through phytoncides, which are compounds released by plants and trees to protect them from insects and infectious agents. When we breathe in phytoncides, they can have immune-modulating, anti-inflammatory and antioxidant effects.

Shinrin-Yoku and additional benefits

The benefits of forest bathing don't stop with our mental wellbeing, cardiovascular system and immune system. Time in nature can reduce pain and improves our health-related quality of life. When we're out in nature, we're usually moving in some way, so we're not being sedentary. If we're in the sun, we're making vitamin D, which is essential for healthy bones, teeth and muscles (although it is very important to use sun protection and not to get burned). In addition to this, we may be spending time with friends, which enhances our social wellbeing.

How to practise forest bathing

Forest bathing is easy and free. In its simplest form, it involves taking a walk in a green area. Interestingly, the studies that have explored forest bathing have all been done under different conditions – for example, for different durations, in different weather and light conditions and with different forest compositions. Although we can't say exactly what the 'best' practice is, the key message is just to get out into the green!

Some places offer guided Shinrin-Yoku experiences, but this absolutely isn't necessary. Some of the best ways to experience the healing power of nature are to:

- Find somewhere quiet without too many people around.
- Slow down. Allow yourself to travel through a forest or other, open, green space, without rushing, so you have time to really see and appreciate what is around you.
- Be mindful. Mindfulness describes being present in the here and now and focusing your attention on the current moment. As you walk through the forest, allow your consciousness to pause on what you experience – the colours, smells, sounds and sensations you encounter.
- Pause. Take the opportunity to stop and allow yourself to focus on one sense in greater detail. Really take note of nature – the sound of a stream, the details in a leaf or the feel of tree bark.
- You may want to have your phone on you in case of any emergencies, but try to keep it turned off and out of sight so you're not distracted. Don't use a camera to take pictures, allow your eyes and mind to be your tool.

There is even some evidence that looking at pictures or videos of forests can have positive effects on our wellbeing, so you could consider changing your screen image to one of trees or finding a room to work in with a green view.

Are other natural environments beneficial?

Absolutely! Although most of the research has explored the beneficial effects of forests, there is evidence that other natural environments are good for us too. For example, exposure to high altitudes and waterfalls has been shown to improve lung function and reduce inflammation in children with asthma. Coastal walks increase feelings of happiness and calmness as well as improve our sleep. When we see or hear bodies of water, such as the sea, this reduces stress levels and helps mental restoration: mindfully looking at the ocean helps us to achieve a meditative state, and the sound of the waves activates our parasympathetic nervous system.

Sue, retired journalist, age 70

I find the natural world a powerful force when it comes to restoring my mental health. For me, little equals the pleasure of suddenly getting a close-up view of a wild creature such as a squirrel or hedgehog. Watching them for a minute or two puts a smile on my face and in my soul. The sound of the waves can smooth the worry lines in my mind and the feel of the sun on my skin is an instant relaxant. All it takes is setting aside the time to soak in the benefits … something I'm not always good at.

Anne, mum of a teenager and lucky owner of a running buddy on four legs

As I tie the laces of my muddy trainers, you wag your tail with enthusiasm. You have been following me since you saw me put on my running socks. I clip your harness to my running belt and off we go to the local woods for another adventure.

Within minutes our senses are flooded by musty smells, tones of green and the muffled sounds of the forest. You drop your nose to the ground, where leaves rest and hold exciting scents. Who was there before you? A deer? Another dog? Dare I say it, a squirrel? You encourage me to increase my pace as we start to run.

I am always amazed by how quickly our surroundings change. My feet hit the ground softly and the earth sends me back up with a gentle push. As we run through the woods, the sun pierces the canopy of leaves and shines through the trees. We are warmed by its rays and guided by its light.

The path unfurls and we reach a dip in the forest, a remnant of the Second World War when bombs created craters in the wood. My mind clears and stresses about 'to do' lists fade away. My lungs fill with fresh air and my back straightens. You look at me with excitement and I forget my worries.

Children have built huts with branches found on the muddy soil. Their rudimentary constructions transform the woods into playgrounds and magical worlds. They remind me of the joyous excitement I experienced swinging above a void when I was on holiday as a child.

Thump, thump, my feet take us a bit further, and we reach a wider path. My shins are covered with scratches from brambles and nettles. The respite of a flat clay track is welcome. Hopefully I won't trip over a root today. The smell in the woods is rich with mulching leaves and a thousand scents that I cannot identify. My nostrils are saturated with a moist rusty aroma. What do you think? What can you smell, with your sensitive nose? You suddenly catch a whiff that is mysterious to me and pull in another direction.

As I listen to the birds, noticing the humming sounds of distant traffic, I catch sight of a tiny rabbit dashing away and I forget about work and daily worries. We are on an adventure just minutes from our doorway. We come out of the wood and jog across the field. Are you ready to go home?

Our run in the woods cleared my head and awoke my body. My limbs are supple, and my face is flushed. I glow and feel energised, ready to face a new day, at peace with myself and with a renewed enthusiasm for whatever I may face. As for you, you stretch your muddy, muscular body across the kitchen floor and go to sleep as I head off to work.

Thank you, world, for letting us enjoy your treasures this morning; I can't wait for tomorrow and our next running adventure in the local woods.

What about the digital environment?

Our digital devices play a huge part in our lives. In the UK, ninety-nine per cent of young adults aged between sixteen and twenty-four years own a smartphone, which we check an average of every twelve minutes when we are awake. Data shows that we spend nearly four hundred minutes a day using the internet, which equates to nearly seven hours. During this time, around two and a half hours are devoted to social media. Social media fuels the reward and addiction circuits of our brains. When we receive 'likes' or comments on our posts, this triggers the release of dopamine, which we have seen in previous chapters acts as a 'feel-good' chemical. Many people find that they mindlessly spend large amounts of time scrolling through their social media apps. The reason for this is usually a subconscious desire for a dopamine hit, but with time, the scrolling becomes a habit, and we do it automatically without really thinking about what we're doing or why.

Whilst enhanced digital connectivity undoubtedly has some benefits, for many people it confers a negative impact on wellbeing.

Digital devices and health

If we consider television and internet time, we spend over forty per cent of our lives attached to our screens. A significant concern is that whilst we're doing this, we're neglecting the activities that actually do us good. We're not moving or exercising. We're not engaging with family and friends in real life. We're not being mindful or spending time in nature.

One of the key ways in which our digital devices are potentially harmful is the impact they have on our sleep. The screens of smartphones, computers and some televisions emit significant amounts of blue light. When we are exposed to this, it suppresses our production of melatonin, which is the hormone that helps us to fall asleep. If we use our electronic items too close to bedtime, this can make us feel alert and wakeful and prevents us from winding down. Our digital devices affect our sleep in other ways as well. We may prioritise watching another episode of our favourite series above going to bed, or we may be woken during the night by notifications from our phone. If we use social media this can keep our minds active, and we can find it hard to 'switch off' to achieve a restful state, which we need to nod off.

The impact that social media and other forms of screen time have on our mental wellbeing is inconclusive. On the one hand, it is easy to see how it could be harmful. Posts on social media are usually carefully curated – we show our best selves and may use filters to enhance the appearances of our lives. This gives an unrealistic picture of normality. For some people, comparison to such images can lead to feelings of inadequacy and poor self-esteem. However, the research that has explored this hasn't come to a definitive conclusion.

'Heavy' users of digital media, who are online for five or more hours a day, have been found to be more unhappy, to have a lower sense of wellbeing and to feel more depressed than 'light' users, who spend less than an hour daily on their digital devices. Some reports state that social media has an adverse effect on work, home life and social life, and that high levels of use may worsen self-esteem, perceived isolation and anxiety about health. Studies have even found that the mere presence of a mobile phone can impair the relationship between strangers. However, more recent research did not replicate this finding. There are reports that screen time, especially television viewing, may impair physical and cognitive development, and may cause obesity, sleep problems, depression and anxiety.

In contrast, other groups have found that moderate use of digital technology is not intrinsically harmful or that the effect is extremely small. One study described certain social media platforms as having a positive association with self-esteem, being extraverted, narcissism, life satisfaction, social support and resilience.

The impact of screen time at an individual level is likely to be dependent on several factors including the age of the user, the length of time spent on devices, the time of day that social media is accessed, baseline levels of self-esteem and self-confidence, support networks and whether individuals are passive 'scrollers' or active participants online. Strategies to help us to use our digital devices safely are outlined below:

- **Assess your screen time**. Many of us use our smartphones for much longer periods than we might realise. It can be helpful to understand our digital patterns so that we can consider whether we want to make any changes. Ironically, this information can often be provided by your phone. You can see your total screen time, and this can be broken down into the time spent on each app. When I did this, the insight horrified me!
- **Set yourself limits**. Think about how long it is acceptable to be using your device. Many electronic items allow you to set time limits, so you get sent a warning or are logged off when your time is up.
- **Don't have screen time in the two to three hours before you go to bed**. This is important when we're trying to optimise our sleeping patterns. If you need to use your devices in the evening, consider putting them into 'night mode' or investing in a pair of glasses that block blue light.

- **Turn off as many notifications as possible**. Notifications often act as a trigger for you to check your device. It can be useful to turn them off so that you have more control of your actions. You *choose* when you look at your device rather than it prompting you to do so.
- **Put your phone in another room**, especially if you want to concentrate on something or to remain focused.
- **Don't follow social media accounts which have a negative impact on you**, focus on those which inspire you.
- **Try not to scroll as a habit**, use social media selectively and with intention.
- **Consider having a screen-free day each week, or a digital detox for a longer time period**. I tried this a few years ago and it had a profound impact on me. I am now far more mindful of how I use my phone and it has much less grip on my attention. My experience is described in Box 1.

Summary

Social media and the internet undoubtedly have their benefits – they allow the world to become more connected, they permit easy sharing of knowledge and can bring together like-minded individuals. But, as human beings, we are community creatures. A hug will do you more good than receiving a 'like' on a post, and cooking for a friend will bring you more joy than photographing a healthy meal.

Sometimes it can be important to take stock of your life, to consider how you are spending your time, and what habits you may be passing on to future generations. Would you rather your children played a game of tag with you or saw you giving kudos on Strava? We know that actions speak louder than words, so it can be helpful to consider what actions you do that other people could model.

BOX 1: MY SOCIAL MEDIA STORY

My alarm goes off and the first thing I do is check my phone. Inevitably there are notifications from Facebook, Instagram, WhatsApp and Strava. I have emails to read and messages to reply to. I'm compelled to respond to 'likes' and comments. My mind is active, and I already feel hassled by some of the more complex messages which need a comprehensive reply. For some ridiculous reason, I'm conscious that the pace of my last run was slower than usual, and that my running followers may think I'm not as fit as I actually am. Why on earth would that matter?

All this before 6.30 am. I haven't even said 'good morning' to my husband.

I have a shower, then feel the need to check my phone again, just in case anything has happened in the last ten minutes.

'Mummy come and look at this,' one of my daughters cries excitedly.

'I'll be there in a second darling, I just have an important message to send' is my shameful response. I suddenly question when it became acceptable that texting was more important than real-life family interactions? I strongly believe that the answer to this is that it isn't. I want to be there for my family, in body and in mind. I don't want to be a digitally distracted mum and wife.

To me, it seems that social media has got an unhealthy grip on society. We are a nation of digital addicts, communicating through our screens rather than taking the time to nourish relationships in person. I know I am guilty of this. It is something I have acknowledged before and have wanted to change, but the draw of the blue screen always entices me back.

I decided to monitor my social media usage throughout the day to gain a greater understanding of the impact it was really having on my life. I drive to work, and as soon as I park my car, my phone is out of my bag. I scroll through Facebook posts as I walk to my office. During my breaks, I obsessively look at my phone. I reply to a random stream of messages about school trips, a pub quiz, running challenges and the car's MOT. I'm sent photos of a friend's lunch (which looked very tasty) and another friend's holiday (she'd met puffins). A friend wants to come over this evening for a coffee before she goes away for the weekend and I plan how I'm going to travel to my next half-marathon. As I walk back to the car, I notice a beautiful flower. My first thought is what meaningful statement I could make about it on Instagram.

On the drive home, I stop for petrol and I check my phone. I get to my house and respond to emails and text messages the second I park. Thankfully, during dinner, I have some digital respite, as we have a family rule that electronic devices are not allowed at the table.

Throughout the evening, my phone is an extension of my arm. I mindlessly stare at the screen as I run the bath, as I'm on the toilet, as I walk between rooms. I'm not doing anything vaguely productive, but am captured by photos of strangers' meals, posts about how to stop washing machines smelling and images of people I'll never meet.

Even more concerningly, I become aware of the unhealthy influence that this is having on me and my wellbeing. I'm just about to turn 40 and I have a healthy weight, a resting heart rate of less than sixty beats per minute and a fitness age of a 20-year-old (so my fitness app tells me). I exercise at least four times a week and can run a half-marathon without a second thought. So why is it that I feel I should be doing more? I feel I need to lose weight and tone up. I think I should be stronger, faster and more supple. I feel guilty that I'm not doing yoga, Pilates, CrossFit and weights to supplement my running.

I work as a doctor in the NHS and have a PhD in cancer genetics, but even that seems inadequate. I feel I should also be getting qualified in nutrition. I'm not sure why though.

Social media is also causing me to spend more. The pages I look at are interspersed with targeted advertisements for products I like. I find myself ordering some new activewear, even though I have far too many pairs of leggings already. My activewear addiction is a bit of a joke amongst my running friends.

As I get into bed, my phone tells me that my screen time has been three hours and thirty-three minutes. This is over a fifth of my waking hours. Over a year, this would amount to over 1200 hours, nearly fifty-four whole days and nights. What a waste of precious time.

Frankly, writing this horrified me. It highlighted the amount of headspace, time, energy and money that I was wasting as a result of social media. I made the decision to have a digital detox. To spend a month (mostly) screen-free.

Although I wanted to go cold turkey, this was not possible as I was running an online charity fitness event. So, I weaned myself gradually. First, I removed myself from any unnecessary WhatsApp groups and turned off notifications. This alone was surprisingly empowering. I was in control of when I chose to look at messages, rather than being constantly bombarded with bleeps and flashing screen reminders. I then deleted Instagram from my phone. Almost immediately my mindset felt as though it had shifted. I was able to appreciate things for what they were in the here and now, as opposed to seeing them through a virtual lens and filter, associated with wise words and hashtags.

Over the next week, I made several more changes. I changed my Strava settings so that my runs were only visible to myself, which was rather timely as a friend told me she had been analysing my heart rate when I ran. To be honest it made me feel rather uncomfortable that I was being scrutinised to such a great extent. I felt very exposed.

I turned off notifications for Facebook and set myself a social media screen-time limit of thirty minutes a day. I let everyone know what I was doing so that if I was delayed in responding to messages or missed any important posts they would understand why.

And so, my holiday from the screen began.

FOUR WEEKS LATER

I'm actually writing this three months later, as life has hurtled along at such a great pace that this is my first opportunity to sit and write. My digital detox was a turbulent journey. I found the first week incredibly difficult. Paradoxically, I looked at my screen even more than usual. It was like being on a diet – as soon as you want to lose weight, all you can think about is food. Because I wasn't receiving notifications about messages, I didn't know when they had arrived, so I kept compulsively checking for them. Although I had limited my social-networking time, I would press the 'ignore' option to keep browsing.

I realised that my good intentions were not being followed through, so I had a stern word with myself. My screen usage had become such an ingrained habit that breaking it required a conscious effort each and every day. I put my phone on silent, and I placed it face down on the desk when I was at work so that the screen wasn't visible. I would only allow myself to look at it at certain times of the day and only for defined periods.

The benefits of reduced digital activity soon became apparent. One of the first things I became aware of was that my concentration span markedly improved. I could complete tasks more efficiently and productively without a continual need to look at my mobile device. More importantly, I noticed that my interactions with family, friends and colleagues became more meaningful. It didn't matter what the topic of conversation was – I was enjoying genuinely engaging with real people rather than half listening to stories and tales, whilst browsing online.

I was more satisfied with my life and what I have now, and my previous need to take on more activities, tasks and duties faded. I could appreciate things in the present to a much greater extent, and my whole outlook became more mindful. My bank balance benefitted from reduced spending … I was no longer exposed to so many adverts, so my desires to buy unnecessary items disappeared.

Overall, my digital detox had a profound and positive effect on my quality of life. My relationships improved, my concentration improved and unnecessary financial spending reduced. I became more grateful, and I spent more quality time with real-life family and friends.

Relationships and Social Connections
Dr Sonal Shah and Rupal Shah

Human beings are social creatures and the relationships we have with our friends, family members and colleagues play a major role in our health and wellbeing. As early as 1624, the English poet John Donne wrote that 'no man is an island' and the significance of this has really been highlighted throughout the pandemic, when countless people have suffered from the effects of social isolation. We are hardwired to belong and to be part of society as a whole. Donne believed that we are 'a piece of the continent' and we therefore cannot function in isolation. Being part of a bigger picture is what helps to form our sense of humanity.

Human beings need to belong

Humans need a safe and secure environment, and we need to share this with other people. Our drive to feel a sense of belonging is a fundamental part of who we are. Historically, when we lived as part of a tribe, we relied on other tribe members for our survival. If we were alone, we were susceptible to attack from predators or starvation. The human brain has evolved to seek out companionship.

Throughout most of evolution, our need for social connections has been strong. We have lived surrounded by family and as part of communities. But, over the last several decades, this structure has been eroded. Many family members now live apart from each other as individuals move around for work or to study, and there is less community cohesion and support. The rise in prominence of the internet has meant that many people have an increased dependence on 'virtual friends' and spend more time on their screens than interacting with people in real life. Traditional models of employment have become more flexible, and there are more opportunities for individuals to work from home, therefore eliminating the opportunity to engage with others in the workplace.

Being disconnected is harmful – studies have shown that loneliness has the same impact on our health as smoking fifteen cigarettes a day and increases the risk of depression, anxiety, heart disease, stroke and early death. As humans, we have a 'hierarchy of needs' – a sense of belonging follows food, water, rest and a safe environment as a necessity in allowing us to exist and flourish:

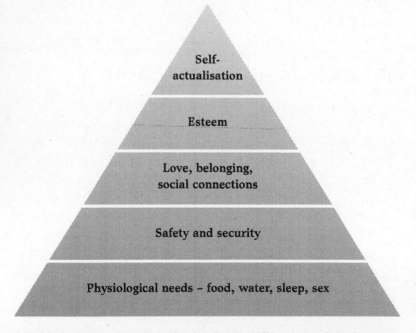

Maslow's hierarchy of needs: fundamentally we need food, water, sleep and sex to survive. Once these needs are met, we can attend to needs higher up in the pyramid.

The need for social connections is present throughout our entire life, from childhood to old age. For many people, relationships are felt to be meaningful when they provide support, encouragement and make us feel valued. Positive relationships are one of the most important factors in shaping wellbeing. UK data has shown that those who are married or in a civil partnership have higher levels of life satisfaction, a greater feeling that life is worthwhile and higher levels of happiness than those who are cohabiting, single, divorced or widowed.

What are 'friends'?

Throughout our lives we have many different social encounters, and our interactions occur on a variety of different levels – from the bus conductor with whom we exchange superficial pleasantries, to the colleague we recount our weekend adventures to, to the friend we share our most intimate secrets with. All of these different encounters are important to our sense of wellbeing, and this holds true for almost all personality types.

There are several different psychological and social theories about what forms the foundation of a friendship or relationship. To put it simply, a friend is someone you like, someone you enjoy spending time with and someone with whom you have a positive relationship. Friends are good for us; they are people we have fun with. They can lift us if we're feeling down, and they can be a sounding post to bounce ideas off. The best friendships are ones which are mutually beneficial and equal. Having good friends staves off loneliness.

Some evolutionary psychologists have suggested that our brains can only manage to deal with around one hundred and fifty friendships, and this is related to how much time and energy we have to share. However, within this number, our relationships vary in intimacy. Some people have a central group of three to five very close friends with whom they have significant, deep and meaningful connections. Beyond that, as the numbers in the 'circle' increase, our closeness and connections generally become less important:

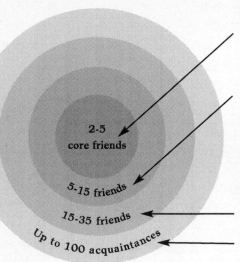

Deep and meaningful connections, fundamental to our wellbeing

Important social support, we enjoy spending time with them and make an effort to see them regularly

We enjoy their company and talking to them, but tend not to make an effort to socialise outside of situations we encounter them by chance

This can include members of our extended family

2-5 core friends

5-15 friends

15-35 friends

Up to 100 acquaintances

Loneliness

When humans lack social connections, we can experience loneliness. This is a complex human emotion, describing a state of solitude and is different to being 'alone'. Loneliness is a feeling that can be experienced by people of all ages, backgrounds and from countries around the world. Many people are able to live alone but not feel lonely. On the other hand, being surrounded by people doesn't stop someone from experiencing loneliness.

Loneliness is a perceived social isolation, and people feel discontent with the *quality* of their relationships rather than their *quantity*. Many personal, social and circumstantial factors can play a role in causing someone to feel lonely. Loneliness is the social equivalent of physical pain, hunger or thirst.

When we are socially isolated or feel lonely, this heightens our inbuilt 'vigilance' for potential threats, which means that we focus our attention on the negative aspects of our lives. In the short term, loneliness can create a psychological desire to 'reconnect' with others. In the same way that hunger makes us seek food, feeling alone makes us seek the 'protection' of a group. However, in the long term, persistent feelings of negativity resulting from being lonely can result in a reduction in social interactions and further social isolation. We feel lonely, so we withdraw, which makes us feel even more lonely. The self-reinforcing loneliness loop is accompanied by feelings of hostility, stress, pessimism, anxiety and low self-esteem. When we are continually in a state of 'high vigilance' this is associated with activation of our sympathetic or 'stress' nervous system, chronic inflammation and poor sleep.

Many negative physical and mental health conditions are linked to loneliness. These conditions can lead to suicide and can even be the root cause of traffic accidents. When we don't feel as though we belong, we can experience premature death at a rate similar to that caused by obesity and smoking. We can also experience poor appetite, fatigue and depression. There is evidence that experiences of 'social pain', from rejection or isolation, activate the same brain regions that are usually involved in the experience of physical pain, which means that loneliness can actually 'hurt'.

How do we become socially connected?

So, in the modern world, how do we nurture and develop our social ties? In the 1990s, the 'belongingness hypothesis' suggested that:

'much of what human beings do is done in the service of belongingness'.

It was proposed that *any* meaningful connection is good for us, rather than just the close relationships that we might have with friends or family. It suggested that the connections we have must occur frequently and must be pleasurable, for example, they could include the chats we have with the shopkeepers we get to know, and we must feel as though we are mutually bonding rather than the interaction being one-sided.

There are many opportunities for us to enhance our connections. For some people, this comes naturally, but many others find it harder. At the simplest level, we can begin by simply making eye contact and smiling at others. We can take this one step further and make a conscious effort to greet people we pass when we're out walking, or we can spend a few minutes talking to those who serve us in cafes or deliver our parcels.

For the deeper, more significant relationships, it's really important that we are our true self and that we feel comfortable in being open and honest. Authentic relationships require our time and energy, so we must prioritise spending quality time with the people we care about. It's worth taking the time to consider which of your friends you feel a significant connection with so that you can nurture and develop your relationship with them.

If you feel you don't have many friends or any meaningful relationships, opportunities to connect with others might include joining a community group, volunteering, or starting a new hobby.

With any relationship, it's always important to know where your boundaries lie and to make sure that the relationship is fair. In social situations, people are generally 'initiators' or 'acceptors'. Initiators suggest and make the plans – they invite you for a coffee, suggest dinner or book the cinema trip. There are many reasons why people are initiators. They may have high levels of motivation and organisation skills, they may be doing it out of habit, personality type, they may be an extravert or they may want to make others feel valued. Some people thrive from being an initiator, but for many, if their efforts aren't reciprocated, it can lead to feelings of fatigue, exhaustion, resentment and being undervalued. If you have experienced any of this as an initiator, some options might be to:

- take a step back. Pause and reflect on which relationships are important to you and which you want to invest your energy in.
- be honest. Sometimes people are happy for you to always make the plans as they haven't got the confidence to do some themselves or because it's become the norm. You could say something along the lines of 'I'd love to see you over the next month, but I haven't got the headspace to make the arrangements. Could you suggest something?'
- accept that being the initiator can be positive as you're often the 'social glue' for a group.

We can help to make others feel valued by being the one who suggests a meet-up and by making a firm commitment to them. It can be easy to say 'we must have a coffee/catch up', but the words are empty if we don't follow it through. For example, instead of saying 'we should have lunch soon' try 'would you like to meet for lunch on Tuesday at 1 pm at The Café'.

Human beings are social creatures. We have an innate need to connect with others. When we're hoping to improve our health and wellbeing, it's vital that we look beyond the 'traditional' pillars of nutrition and exercise and also prioritise relationships and belonging. Not only will this benefit ourselves, but it will have a positive impact on others and on society as a whole.

Goal Setting and Habits

Dr Emma Short and Dr Aria Campbell-Danesh

Human beings are creatures of habit. Many of our behaviours are carried out automatically without conscious decision making. Our daily habits have a huge impact on our mental and physical wellbeing and affect behaviours such as how active we are or what we eat. If we make a conscious decision to 'become healthier' it is incredibly important to define our goals and to consider what we want to achieve. We might decide:

- I want to be able to walk up a flight of stairs without feeling breathless.
- I want to reduce my risk of developing diabetes.
- I want to improve my sleeping patterns.
- I want to lose five kilograms.
- I want to feel more connected with other people.
- I want to reduce my stress levels.

When we set ourselves goals it helps to motivate us and plan the actions we will take to reach our desired outcome. Once we have our goal in mind, we can turn our attention to what changes we need to make to move us closer to achieving that goal. The process of carrying out these changes is described as 'goal striving'. Ultimately, we hope that these new behaviours will become established as healthy habits.

Goal Setting

When we're setting health and wellbeing goals, it's helpful to be aware that there are different types of goals. These can vary in how easy they are to achieve and the impact that they have on our motivation and confidence levels. The different types of goals are outcome vs process goals, approach vs avoidance goals and challenging vs easy goals. These will be explained below:

Outcome and process goals

Outcome goals describe the desirable 'end results' we want to see, such as five kilograms weight loss. Process goals, on the other hand, are the behaviours or actions that we need to carry out to take us towards our chosen outcome. These might include cooking healthy meals or taking part in a fitness class. Both types of goals are important. However, when we focus our attention on process goals, we are more likely to increase our confidence in our ability to accomplish the goal and to enjoy the changes that we have made. This can help us to stick with our new behaviours. When we develop new skills and habits that promote a healthier lifestyle, we are likely to persevere through any setbacks that arise.

Approach and avoidance goals

An approach goal is something positive that you do that moves you nearer your goals, for example, going for a walk every morning if you want to increase your activity levels. In contrast to this are avoidance goals, which describe cutting out or avoiding something undesirable, such as highly processed foods. Approach goals focus on success and achievement whereas avoidance goals emphasise avoiding failure. If we place our attention and energy on approach goals, we feel more optimistic and satisfied with the progress we make.

Challenging and easy goals

A commonly used framework for goal setting is the SMART framework, which is something that we've mentioned in this book. SMART goals are Specific, Measurable, Achievable, Realistic and Time-bound. Research generally supports the recommendation that *process* goals should be achievable but also challenging for the individual. For example, if someone who is already reasonably active wants to get even fitter, it would be better to suggest going for a jog rather than a walk. Interestingly, some people find that 'unrealistic' *outcome* goals are the most helpful. For instance, when it comes to losing weight, ambitious outcome goals can motivate us to take even greater actions. When we see the numbers on the scale start to drop, this can encourage and motivate us to carry on with new, healthy behaviours, and there is evidence that higher weight-loss targets lead to greater weight loss overall. A very important point though is not to set goals that we find overwhelming or demoralising, as they can stall healthy changes before they've even begun.

In short, if we want to set health-related goals, it can be helpful to have a challenging overall outcome goal, and we work towards it by setting easier, approach-driven process goals:

1 Set an overarching outcome goal that you find inspiring, motivating and personally meaningful.
2 Create smaller, realistic process goals that you can implement into your life now and that will develop the skills you need to move towards your desired end result.
3 Review your process goals to check that they are specific, measurable, time-bound, and approach-oriented. A good tip is that avoidance goals can be converted into approach goals, for instance, eating fewer packets of crisps can be transformed into snacking on hummus and red-pepper slices.

Examples of such goals are listed in Table 1.

TABLE 1: GOAL SETTING

Outcome goal	Process goals	What not to do
Reduce stress levels	Practise mindfulness Prioritise rest	Don't go on social media (avoidance goal)
Improve sleeping patterns	Exercise daily in the morning Have a warm bath in the evening	Rigidly count the number of hours sleep that you achieve (unhelpful outcome goal)
Lose weight	Eat healthily Regular exercise	Focus on banning chocolate (avoidance goal)

Goal Striving

Goal striving is what we need to do in order to translate our ideals into actions and achievement. Two key types of plan can be helpful in keeping us on track. These are action plans and coping plans.

Action Plans

Action plans involve specifying the what, where, how often and when of new health-related actions. They can be thought of as a detailed version of a SMART goal, for example:

'I will go for a fifteen-minute walk around the local park after breakfast every day for the next week.'

When forming your own action plan, it's important that you:

- take ownership so that specific actions will fit in with your interests and lifestyle;
- make the plan short-term initially, for instance, lasting seven days;

- evaluate the plan after a specified time and adapt it accordingly;
- feel confident that you can actually implement the plan.

An example might be:

- **Date**: Week commencing 19th July
- **Action**: Yoga
- **Duration**: forty-five minutes
- **Location**: Yoga studio
- **Frequency**: Twice a week
- **Days/times**: Wednesday 6.15 pm, Saturday 9.00 am
- **Confidence in accomplishing the plan**: 8/10
- **Observations or insights (including difficulties or barriers)**: Woke up on Sunday feeling exhausted after a busy week and wanted to have a lie-in. Next week I will book the 11.15 am class so I can sleep for longer. Check if Sally wants to go to the same class – accountability will help.

Coping Plans

While action plans tend to *initiate* behaviour change, coping plans help to *maintain* behaviour change. When trying to engage in healthier habits, there will be obstacles, temptations and distractions that risk interfering with your good intentions. Setbacks are a natural part of the process of changing our behaviours and can provide valuable feedback. When things seem to go wrong, your mind may tell you that you have failed and are back at square one. However, you are actually one step ahead because you now have more data to guide you. For instance, you may have planned to spend less time on social media but have ended up scrolling whenever you're bored. If you reflect on your screen time and come to the realisation that boredom triggers digital habits, you can use this information to plan alternative strategies. The key is to be self-compassionate and problem solve your way forward.

Coping plans allow us to identify potential barriers so that we can devise possible solutions. Research shows that using coping and action plans is more powerful than action plans alone. Helpful coping strategies include visualisation and 'if then' plans.

Visualisation

Imagining and mentally playing out the sequence of events leading up to, during and after the desirable action is a useful technique. For instance, you may be trying to drink less alcohol, but you want to go out for dinner with friends who usually drink a lot. When you visualise the event, you may see your friends encouraging you to drink and you're finding it hard to say no. At this stage, think about what you could do in order to stick to your intentions. How would you feel if you drank the alcohol? How would you feel if you stuck to soft drinks? If you know that you wouldn't drink and drive, you could be the designated driver for the night and take your car to the restaurant. Visualisation works hand in hand with 'if then' planning.

If-then plans

Another evidence-based tool to have in your coping planning kit is an *if-then plan*, which is a plan with structure: 'if situation x happens, then I will do y.' For example:

- If my work call overruns and I miss my exercise class, then I will do a 20-minute home YouTube workout.
- If the dessert menu is offered at the restaurant, then I will decline it and order a coffee instead.

Deciding in advance what you will do when faced with a tricky situation creates a link in your brain between a specific context and the desirable behaviour. This connection can be strengthened by writing it down and mentally repeating the association in your head. The situation arising (being offered the dessert menu) will then automatically trigger the pathway in the brain ending in the goal-aligned action (ordering a coffee).

If-then plans should also be approach-oriented and focused on a positive action rather than a negative, avoidance-oriented one. Research shows that plans such as: 'if I start to crave chocolate biscuits, then I will not eat any' tend to be ineffective. A more effective plan would be: 'if I start to crave chocolate biscuits, then I'll have a banana instead.'

I have used this technique successfully when I was trying to eat more healthily. Although I always pack a healthy lunch to take into work, we have a big box of chocolate biscuits within easy reach. Late in the afternoon I would often feel tired and would crave a sugar rush. More often than not I would give in and enjoy the sweet treats. When I decided to minimise my intake of processed foods, my 'if then' plan was to eat a handful of cashews whenever the sugar cravings hit. Before long, I had broken my habit of biscuit eating, and I genuinely no longer wanted them.

Although the techniques of visualisation and 'what if' planning seem very simple, they have been proven to be effective in promoting healthy eating habits, higher physical activity levels, and drinking less alcohol. Some additional examples are given in Box 2.

BOX 2: EXAMPLES OF 'WHAT IF' PLANS

- If my gym buddy cancels attending a class with me, I'll go by myself anyway.
- If someone offers me a glass of wine, I'll ask for a glass of sparkling water.
- If I find that I don't enjoy the yoga class, I'll give Pilates a try instead.
- If I haven't got time to prepare a packed lunch to take to work, I'll have a jacket potato in the canteen rather than chips.

Motivation

Motivation is what drives our actions. It's the force that encourages and inspires us to go for a swim or to stop smoking. Interestingly, there's a difference in the motivation that causes us to start something and the motivation that keeps us going.

We may be driven to take new actions based on a sensible long-term goal. After a loved one has had a stroke, we may decide to lower the amount of salt in our diet. However, rational goals may be insufficient in *maintaining* healthy lifestyle changes. Harnessing the power of intrinsic motivation, enjoyment and the satisfaction linked with new behaviours is vital to long-term success.

Intrinsic motivation

Intrinsic motivation describes doing something because we find it enjoyable or interesting. Even if we don't receive any external rewards for doing it, we carry out the action because it gives us joy. We might read a book about history because we are interested in the world rather than because we have an exam to pass, or we may learn to dance for the happiness of moving to music rather than to put on a show. This is different to extrinsically motivated actions, which are based on external factors such as attention, approval and acceptance from others. Examples include learning to play football because it makes your parents happy or losing weight to please your partner or doctor. Research shows that intrinsically motivated goals lead to greater learning, performance, persistence and progress than extrinsically motivated goals.

Enjoyment and satisfaction

This may seem obvious, but we're more likely to continue healthy behaviours that we genuinely enjoy or that provide an immediate feeling of satisfaction afterwards. If you enjoy playing tennis, then book a regular court slot. If you don't like high-intensity workouts, then don't feel pressured to adopt the latest trend. The key is to find activities that you love, either for the pure joy of doing them or the immediate satisfaction that they give, such as the post-exercise endorphin rush. In short:

Enjoyment + Satisfaction = Sustainability

Habits

As humans, our psychological resources are limited. If a new, healthy behaviour requires continuous and conscious effort, we are likely to become fatigued and slip back into our old, unhealthy ways. That is why it is so important to establish healthy habits – to get to the point at which we carry out healthy behaviours without consciously thinking about them.

Our habits are the actions we routinely repeat in certain situations or in response to certain cues, for example, washing our hands after we have been to the toilet. The strength of a habit increases the more times it is repeated. If someone has had a cigarette every time they have gone to the pub for many years, they will tend to light up automatically the next time they visit their local.

Habits often have two effects on behaviour. The first is that certain environments can trigger certain actions, such as that described in the example relating to smoking. The second is that habits can become stronger than conscious intentions which means that individuals may have automatically smoked in the pub (before it was made illegal) even though they knew it was bad for their health and they wanted to stop. It can therefore be difficult to change a long-established pattern of behaviour.

Many health goals will require breaking old habits and forming new ones. For instance, you may choose to cut out processed sugars and increase your vegetable intake. To achieve this goal, you will need to make a behaviour change and repeat the new behaviour over time.

The formation of a new habit involves three stages, which are:

Initiation phase: Making the decision to take action and then taking that initial action.
Learning phase/repetition: Repetition of the behaviour in the same context/environment, which is often the most difficult step and requires continued motivation and self-regulation.
Stability phase: By repeating the action in a way that helps it to become automatic, the action is now habitual and will occur with minimal effort.

Some people suggest that habits can be established in twenty-one days, but it is more likely there is a wider window, ranging from eighteen to two hundred and fifty-four days. Generally, it is easier to build a simple habit, such as eating a banana each day, than a more complex habit, for example, driving to the gym to do an exercise class. There are, however, some strategies that can be helpful in habit formation:

- **Link your identity with the outcome you want to achieve**, for example, 'I am fit'. Our sense of identity describes how we see ourselves and is related to our values, beliefs, morals, ethics, achievements, the challenges we have faced and our views of the world. Importantly, our sense of identity, whether at a conscious or subconscious level, affects our behaviours, so if we identify as being fit, we are likely to perform actions that fulfil this self-perception.
- **Choose actions that are easy**. Most people automatically choose the path of least resistance. They carry out actions that are simple to do and which require minimal effort. This knowledge can be harnessed to our advantage – making the healthy choice the easy choice. For example, if there is a bowl of fresh fruit on display on the kitchen table, we are more likely to eat an apple than if the fruit bowl is hidden in a cupboard. If we have planned to go for an early morning run,

it can be helpful to leave our gym kit by the door so we don't have to go searching for shorts when our alarm goes off. In the same way, we are less likely to carry out unhealthy actions if they are hard to do. If our phone is in a different room, it is less probable that we will waste time scrolling than if our phone is next to us. Studies have shown that if food is less accessible, we reduce our snack consumption.

- **Do activities that you enjoy**. You are more likely to stick to a new habit if it is something that gives you satisfaction or pleasure.
- **Be patient**. In modern society, most people have become used to instant gratification. When we post on social media we immediately receive 'likes'. When we want to watch a certain TV episode, it's immediately available to view. Humans are hardwired to seek instant pleasure. However, this often isn't compatible with health-related goals. Whilst we may receive short-term gratification from eating a chocolate bar, this might not be consistent with a long-term goal of weight loss. There are many health-related goals which require time and perseverance. These include improving our fitness levels, losing weight, establishing meaningful relationships and building self-confidence. It's therefore crucial that we recognise at the outset that we need to be patient and to see our healthy habits as a lifestyle change rather than a quick fix. It's great to celebrate our achievements, however small they are, as this will help to enhance our motivation to carry on our health journey.

In summary, changing our behaviours and adopting healthy habits can sometimes be challenging. However, if we set goals, focus on the process of achieving these goals and celebrate our successes, this can help bring us closer to our desired outcome.

When aiming to make healthier choices, the following tips can be useful:

- **Think about** *why* **you want to make a change.** You are much more likely to achieve your goals if your motivation has come from within yourself rather than from other people telling you what you should do. You need to *want* to make a change.
- **Ensure you plan well,** including 'what if' plans.
- **Perform new behaviours in a specific environment so that the environment becomes the trigger for the action.** For example, every time you go to the canteen for a lunch break, choose an apple rather than a packet of crisps so the canteen becomes a trigger for healthy eating.
- **Monitor your behaviour.** This allows you to identify any discrepancies between what you have planned to do and what you are actually doing. You can then use this information to modify your actions if necessary. You will also be able to see your achievements, which is rewarding and provides positive, motivating feedback.
- **Repeat, repeat, repeat healthy behaviours.** It is known that habits result from repeating actions in certain environments. It is therefore vitally important that you repeat new behaviours so they become automatic and you don't have to make a conscious decision to perform them.
- **To break unhealthy habits, disrupt the cue pattern.** This involves avoiding the environments which trigger the behaviour and also self-programming to carry out different behaviours in those environments. If we revisit the smoking example, an individual could try to avoid going to the pub, but if they do go, they could chew a piece of gum rather than have a cigarette.

Although humans are creatures of habit, we are conscious beings, and we have the power to use our consciousness to assess our behaviours and to make changes for the better.

Ideas, Mindset and Stress Reduction

Dr Emma Short

Our minds and our bodies are intimately linked so anything which impacts one will affect the other. When we begin our journey of improving our health, it's easy to focus on our physical wellbeing. We might aim to increase our fitness or lose weight. However, it's just as important to look after our mental health and to consider how we can improve our mental wellbeing. One of the major ways in which we can do this is to reduce our stress levels, which is one of the fundamental pillars of Lifestyle Medicine. I also believe that to thrive and be happy it is important to have a positive mindset and to focus our attention on the good in the world.

In this chapter, we'll take a look at what stress is, and we'll explore how to reduce our stress levels by not overcommitting to too many activities and responsibilities. We will consider the positive effects that meditation and mindfulness can have on wellbeing, and we'll delve into how the practices of gratitude and kindness can foster a positive mindset.

Stress

Our stress response occurs when we detect a potentially dangerous threat. This activates a variety of neural and hormonal pathways that allow us to deal with the threat. Throughout evolution, the danger was likely to have been an attack from a predator. Our sympathetic nervous system kicks into action and our cortisol levels rise to allow 'fight or flight' — we fight the enemy, or we run to a place of safety. Once the threat has gone, either because we have won the fight or because we are safely hidden, our stress response settles, and our parasympathetic nervous system is activated to restore us to a state of calm.

Historically, our stress response was therefore activated episodically for short periods of time, but the picture is different in modern life. We no longer face predatory attack, but our stressors can include work deadlines, family fallouts or financial pressures. These can cause continued activation of our stress responses which means we don't get any downtime to recover. We may experience palpitations, feelings of anxiety, heartburn or difficulty sleeping. In the long term, chronic stress increases our risk of heart disease, gastrointestinal problems and mental health disorders. We may find it hard to focus and we can often feel overwhelmed.

Don't do too much: Superwoman, Superman take off your cape

All of us have different sources of stress. It's not possible to address them all in this book, as they are unique to each individual's own set of circumstances. However, it's very common for people to feel stressed because they have taken on too many roles and responsibilities. In modern life, 'being busy' is often worn as a badge of honour, and many people fall victim to 'Superwoman/Superman Syndrome'.

What is Superwoman/Superman Syndrome?

The term 'Superwoman Syndrome' was first coined by the American author, Marjorie Shaevitz in 1984. She wrote that Superwoman is 'extraordinary in that she tries to be everything to everyone – juggling family life, social life and commitments outside the home ... The new Superwoman "has it all" by "doing it all" with superlative standards and ends up feeling overwhelmed, overextended, overworked and underappreciated.'

Most of us know at least one Superwoman or Superman – the person who seems to be able to do it all, excelling in everything they turn their hand to. They're perpetually busy and appear to succeed in all areas of life, with great ease. We may know this person, or we may be them.

When we're 'doing it all' we may be leading a rich and fulfilling life. We might feel confident, capable and as though we're having a positive impact on the world. We may thrive on achieving our goals or on helping others. But being busy can easily tip into being *too busy*, and overcommitting can be detrimental to our wellbeing. There is a balance between leading a rich and varied life and being so stretched that mental and emotional resources are drained. Although we may manage to keep many balls in the air for a while, there often comes a time when we feel as though we're drowning in our 'to do' list.

It's therefore really important to explore the reasons why we overload ourselves. It's only once we understand this that we can think about ways to stop this from happening.

Some of the feelings experienced by those who have overcommitted include irritability, resentment and a feeling of being a failure. It's common to hear that taking on too much can lead to difficulties sleeping, fatigue and exhaustion, unhealthy eating habits and drinking too much alcohol. When our minds are continually active, we can find it hard to focus and may have difficulties 'switching off' at the end of the day.

As Rachel, a 41-year-old doctor and mother of one, says:

> *I know when I'm doing too much as I find it hard to focus and become increasingly distracted. When I'm not at work I'm continually checking my phone and responding to messages, and my evenings are spent organising events. I get incredibly irritable and impatient. A lot of what I do tends to be charity-related or*

supporting other people. It follows a repeating pattern of snowballing out of control then crashing down – I reach the point of feeling angry and resentful that I do so much for other people, but no one cares about me. I often feel used and taken for granted.

And Julie, a 35-year-old mother of two who works in scientific research alongside studying for a degree, states:

I enjoy being busy, and at times the number of responsibilities I have seem to be an enjoyable challenge. More often, however, I feel overwhelmed with everything that needs to be done. Things 'for me' will often get pushed to the bottom of the list, including my study time and time to exercise. I have become anxious in recent months, with interrupted sleep as I worry about things during the night. At its worst, I have had days where I will sit for hours worrying; knowing that I have so much to do and yet unable to complete any one task.

Many of the negative impacts of Superwoman/ Superman Syndrome occur because we are permanently in a state of stress. We take on too many responsibilities and we don't get a break or the opportunity to wind down. When we overcommit, we step out of our comfort zone into the realm of panic.

What causes people to take on too much?

Taking on too many roles can be harmful, and yet countless people around the world find themselves in this situation. The common response is often simply to advise people to do less. There are thousands of articles and books which explore how to achieve a satisfactory work-life balance. Some of these tips are listed in Box 3. While all of these strategies are valid in helping to achieve temporary balance, they are short-term measures as they don't address what is driving individuals to do too much in the first place. Without this understanding, people will not be able to develop their own personal techniques to slow down.

There are many different reasons why we do too much. Most of the time, there are several contributing factors, which we may not even be aware of. These can include our personality type or sense of self-identity, a need for recognition and approval from others or a sense of moral duty to help those less fortunate than ourselves. We may be genuinely passionate and enthusiastic about the opportunities life offers, or we may keep ourselves busy to stay distracted from a painful experience. For some, the buzz of achieving a goal becomes an addiction, and people will continually take on more to get their fix. Others may have a deep lack of self-confidence or a fear of failure and stay busy to 'prove' that they are worthy.

Take the case of Maria, a 42-year-old single mother of two, who works in a senior management role:

> I think there are lots of reasons we take on too much. I think women experience a lot of external conditioning that sets the bar really high. Today's woman needs to be a great mum, domestic goddess, successful at work, care for others, keep herself fit and be great in bed! Alongside that external pressure, I am a very driven person so there's an internal ambition to take things on and always do more. I also feel a moral duty to use my privilege for good – to speak for others, advocate for positive change, contribute to society. I never feel like I'm doing enough on that front, but I have to be really disciplined with myself about not taking on too much at home or at work because the consequence of taking on too much is that instead of giving yourself, you take away from yourself.

It is important to understand why we overcommit, as different driving factors require different strategies to overcome them. The major reasons and targeted techniques we can use to prevent getting overloaded are outlined below:

1   **Personality type and sense of identity.** Our personality describes our unique set of characteristics and traits that make us who we are. Our personality affects our thoughts, feelings and behaviours and results from a complex interplay between our genetics, the environment we were brought up in and our life experiences. There are many different ways of describing or classifying personalities, but one of the best-known ways is that of personality types A–D, in which type A individuals are competitive, ambitious and goal-driven. It is easy to see how those with a type A personality might take on too much – they feel a sense of achievement when they successfully complete tasks and challenges, so they commit to a variety of activities to continually experience their own success. People with type A personality often set very high standards for themselves, so as well as doing a lot, they put a lot of pressure on themselves to do it brilliantly, which can further increase stress levels.

For those who overcommit as a result of their personality type, the first step is to pause before taking on a new task, so that committing doesn't become a habit. It is important for individuals to reflect on what they have already achieved, as past successes easily get forgotten when they're racing through life at full pelt. It is also necessary to consider what really matters to them, to think about when they last experienced joy or contentment. The answers may be surprising – although the achievement of goals gives a temporary ego boost, people often learn that feelings of calm and happiness are experienced in everyday moments away from tasks and 'to do' lists.

Before agreeing to any new commitments, it can be helpful to ask three questions:

1   Will I enjoy this/will it make me happy?
2   Will it be beneficial?
3   Can I do it without it causing unnecessary stress?

The third question is perhaps the most important, but it is also the most frequently neglected. If we consider all three, it can remind us to put the brakes on before we agree to doing more. By taking on less, it also allows more time to work on the tasks we have already started. Time is finite, and if we want to do a job well, we need to be prepared to put the time in. When we're juggling many roles, the time we can commit to each is inevitably less, potentially meaning that tasks aren't completed to the best of our abilities. For those with type A personalities, by doing less we can maintain high standards, which reduces stress levels.

Our sense of identity is related to our personality but is a different concept. It describes how we see ourselves and is related to our values, beliefs, morals, ethics, achievements, the challenges we have faced and our views of the world. Importantly, our sense of identity, whether at a conscious or subconscious level, affects our behaviours, so if we identify as being overly busy, we are likely to perform actions to fulfil this self-perception. In this scenario, we must first draw our awareness to how we see ourselves. Once we understand that our views of ourselves can drive us to overcommit, it becomes easier to break the cycle. Many people find that self-affirmations can help to change our mindset, for example:

- 'I am in control.'
- 'I do not take on too much.'
- 'I take time to consider my own needs.'

2 **Recognition and approval from others.** Unfortunately, all too frequently, many people put others' needs above their own. This often stems from a desire to please others, or a reliance upon other people's approval for a sense of worth. Dr Aria Campbell-Danesh, high-performance psychologist and coach, writes that:

   We are all connected by core human needs. Physical needs include food, water, air and shelter. Once these are met, there are intrinsic psychological drivers that motivate human behaviour. One of the most powerful is the desire for recognition and approval from others.

Humans have an inbuilt need to feel safe and secure. From an evolutionary perspective, our survival depended on being part of a social group. We relied upon others to stay alive, whether through hunting, foraging or protection from predators and the elements. Exclusion from the group literally meant death. We are therefore hardwired to be acutely aware of approval cues to assess the strength of our relationship bonds. Brain scan studies have shown that social rejection actually 'hurts', triggering the same pain areas in the brain that are activated during the experience of physical pain.

In today's world, the evolutionary hangover of seeking recognition and approval from others can have negative consequences. We can become obsessed with appearing impressive and pleasing others. The need for approval can drive us to 'prove' the value that we are adding to the world.

Ironically, attempts to be seen as worthy can elicit or consolidate a subconscious belief that we are not enough as we are. A vicious pattern of working too hard, doing too much for others, ruminating about what others think, and not making adequate time for self-care sets in.

These ideas are echoed by Leah Morantz, Chart.PR, MCIPR, Head of Communications for Public Health Wales NHS Trust. Leah's experience comes from balancing multiple roles – in work, as a parent and as a volunteer:

For most of us, getting recognition from others feels good. Maybe it's praise from your boss on a job well done, a compliment from a friend about your fashion sense or decorating style, or even peer validation from other professionals in your network. Constructive feedback is part of effective work cultures and fosters connection. This external validation can give us a sense of accomplishment, boosting confidence, making us feel seen and appreciated. But there's a danger that we might come to rely solely on this external validation to reinforce our sense of self or confirm for us that we are good enough.

Some people thrive on the validation and recognition they receive for their accomplishments. The problem with this comes when we seek validation from an external source at the expense of building our self-worth from within. After all, external validation isn't guaranteed. When we rely on others for our sense of self-worth, we give power over ourselves to others and their judgement of us.

Consciously shifting the balance of the importance you place on external versus internal validation can be a helpful way to build resilience and focus on positive self-appraisal. Are you good enough? Yes. You are. But it's not important what I think. In the end, the judgement we place on ourselves is the most powerful. If you develop the habit of judging yourself more kindly and focus on the things that you value about yourself, you can let go of how others judge you. You can come to rely on external validation less. You can decide that you are worthy, that you are enough, and you can retain power over yourself, reducing your reliance on outside validation. And for some people, this can free them from the constant desire to please, to achieve, to perform and to make others happy.

Dr Campbell-Danesh describes three practical strategies that can be helpful in overcoming the need for the external validation:

- **Establish and reinforce the belief that you are enough as you are**. Write down the answers to these three questions: *What are my strengths? What do I like about myself? What am I most proud of, personally and professionally?* Read these daily as a constant reminder of who you are.

- **Be true to your values**. It is impossible to keep everyone happy. Sometimes sharing our truth, including how we think, feel and act, will upset others. When you focus too much on an outcome, such as the reactions of others, you can end up procrastinating or holding back saying what you know deep down to be right or true to you. What's far more important is whether your words and actions align with your values. Write down your values. *What's important to you in life? What do you enjoy? How would you like to be remembered?* When you face a difficult decision, our values can be a guide.

- **Lean into the discomfort**. Tolerating the discomfort of placing yourself first or on an equal par with others is an ability that develops with practice. As the saying goes, the comfort zone is a lovely place to be, but nothing beautiful grows there. See if you can develop an encouraging, supportive inner voice when facing the unfamiliar. Remind yourself that when you give yourself permission to look after yourself, you'll have more fuel in the tank to contribute and give to others. Throughout the day, ask yourself: *How can I nourish my mind and body?*

3   **Altruism and moral obligation.** In the world we live in, we are fortunate and privileged if we have safe accommodation, education, food and water, a loving upbringing, good health and if we don't face discrimination. Many people recognise this and want to do what they can to help those who aren't as lucky. This is wonderful, important and is certainly needed, but when we do too much, it can be to the detriment of our own wellbeing, which can leave us too tired and drained to do the good we had set out to do in the first place.

A common phrase I often hear is that 'if I don't do my bit, no one will, and nothing will change'. Whilst this may be true to an extent, it is necessary for individuals to recognise that they can only do so much and that any good deed they carry out, no matter how small, will have a positive impact on the world. In the words of Mother Teresa, 'I alone cannot change the world, but I can cast a stone across the waters to create many ripples'. Once this is accepted, many people describe experiencing 'self-permission' to work within their own boundaries.

4 **Passion and enthusiasm.** Some people display a remarkable passion for life, being inspired and motivated by a variety of activities. They can overcommit through pure enthusiasm and excitement. So long as roles and challenges remain fun and enjoyable, this is great, but sometimes the point is reached at which so many activities are being undertaken that their pleasure is lost, and they become a chore.

When this happens, there is a need to prioritise – to acknowledge that time is limited and to consider which commitments are the most rewarding and are worth continuing, and to assess which could be put on hold or stopped.

5 **Distraction.** Keeping busy can sometimes be a means of avoiding difficult or painful situations – when time and thoughts are occupied by tasks, attention can be kept away from sources of discomfort. These sources are highly variable – ranging from unhappy relationships or problems at work to traumatic events in childhood. When overcommitting is being used as an avoidance technique, this is often at a subconscious level, so initially, an individual must be prepared to examine their reasons for taking on too much and to acknowledge that they may have underlying issues that need processing. There are different ways of addressing underlying issues, and these are highly dependent upon what the issues are. Examples might include ending a relationship, setting boundaries within a relationship, changing jobs, engaging in coaching at work, therapy or counselling.

6 **Addiction and habit**. For some people, being overly busy can become a habit. Dr Athanasios Hassoulas, Cardiff University, explains the reasons for this:

Many people feel overwhelmed by taking on too much, but they follow the same pattern of behaviour over and over again. One reason for this is that our behaviours may be triggered by 'operant conditioning'. This means that they are strengthened or weakened depending on their previous consequences. For example, if we receive praise and respect for 'doing so much' we are likely to repeat similar behaviours in the future.

Achieving a goal also makes us feel good in a physical sense. This results from the release of the 'feel-good' chemical, dopamine, in the brain. Dopamine also plays a role in addiction, and we can become addicted to actions that result in a dopamine hit. The buzz we experience after achieving our goals produces such a powerful sense of accomplishment that we continue to overcommit. The craving to take on new challenges can be very powerful and a 'yes' response may come without conscious thought. It's therefore vital to pause before taking on additional commitments and to take time to consider whether it is sensible to go ahead. Before agreeing to new roles and activities, give yourself the space to fully evaluate whether it is something that you have the time and energy for.

7 **Lack of self-confidence**. Being low in self-confidence and self-esteem can have different effects on individuals. Some people feel unable to take on new challenges as they don't have the self-belief that they will be able to successfully complete them. Others will take on many tasks as a means of trying to 'prove' to themselves that they are capable or worthy.

There are lots of different ways to improve self-esteem. Some of the most helpful strategies include recognising your strengths, using positive self-affirmations, practising gratitude, identifying and challenging negative self-beliefs, being non-judgmental of yourself and the world, practising mindfulness, not comparing yourself to others, investing in positive relationships, being kind to others, value-based living and adopting healthy behaviours such as being physically active, prioritising sleep and eating healthily.

8 **A need to be in control.** Dr Nita Maha, a Bristol-based GP, writes that many people are overburdened because they have a need to be in control and they have difficulties delegating tasks to others:

Asking for help doesn't come easily to a lot of people. Delegation can be challenging as it requires trust in another to complete a task and to complete it to a satisfactory standard. This can be difficult for some individuals, particularly if they feel overloaded in their lives and unable to relax and 'let go'. However, the lack of delegation of tasks and the need to be in control can lead to exhaustion. Some people feel disheartened if they cannot complete their 'to do' list without asking for help and perceive this as a sign of weakness or of failing.

In order to address this, we can learn to develop the skill of delegation. This often requires starting out small – let other people take on the 'less important' tasks. Once we see that others are willing and able to help out and can do so successfully, our trust and confidence in them will grow, and we will be less reluctant to ask them to do more.

My experience of Superwoman Syndrome

Without a doubt, I have a tendency to suffer from Superwoman Syndrome. I am a mum, wife and doctor who used to wear the 'Superwoman' label with pride.

My children are eleven and nine years old. Since becoming a parent I've completed a PhD, passed my final exams to become a pathology consultant and I've qualified as a fitness instructor, personal trainer, run leader and meditation teacher. I've set up a running club, written a textbook and smoothie recipe book and have published many health and fitness articles in a variety of magazines and webpages. I've been to France to volunteer at refugee camps and I've organised numerous events which have raised thousands of pounds for charity. I've baked novelty cakes for friends and family, including two wedding cakes, I was the chair of the school PTA and have completed diplomas in Mindful Nutrition and Shinrin-Yoku. I've organised the class end-of-term gifts for the teachers, I set up an online fitness community which has over two thousand members and I arranged our local Black Lives Matter vigil. I've run an ultramarathon, two marathons and many half-marathons. Life has been extraordinarily busy, and I used to like it that way.

I'm a very driven person, and I feel incredibly fortunate for all that I have. I want to use my abilities and skills to help others. I used to relish people saying to me, 'I don't know how you do it all', and I enjoyed being seen as a 'nice person'. I prided myself on excelling in all domains and in continually being on the go.

Although I could see no harm in taking on so many responsibilities and challenges, they were taking their toll. A few years ago, I started to experience palpitations, which led to investigations by a cardiologist. These revealed I was having multiple ventricular ectopics, or extra heartbeats, a known cause of which is stress.

At that time, I made the decision to try to do less. I slowed down for a few months, but before long I was back to my old ways. When life got hectic again, I started to lose my hair. It would fall out in clumps in the shower, resulting in a bald patch on the crown of my head. Although my consciousness hadn't acknowledged I needed to rest, my body was sending me clear messages.

It was around the time that the Covid-19 pandemic hit that I was forced to put on the brakes. I couldn't lead any fitness sessions or club runs, there were no races and my textbook had gone to the printers so didn't need any additional work. There were no school activities and no social events. I was able to spend many hours with my husband and daughters – we walked in the parks, rode our bikes, baked and snuggled watching films. I began to appreciate that this was the life that made me truly happy, that being an overachiever did not define my worthiness.

I came to the realisation that if I wanted to carry on living a calmer and happier life, I needed to understand what had driven me to be so busy in the first place. I needed to reflect on and consider why I felt the need to continually set new goals. Without understanding this, it would have been all too easy to get caught up, yet again, in the trap of 'doing it all'.

I have learned that I overcommit for several different reasons. It is something I do out of habit, and I usually don't consider the impact that being too busy will have on me. I am genuinely passionate and enthusiastic about life, and I like to be continually learning and active. I also feel that I am in a very fortunate position, and I want to do all I can to help other people. In addition to this, being goal-oriented is a part of my personality.

I think that society has glorified being busy, and many people wear it as a badge of honour. However, always being active can lead to fatigue, exhaustion and burnout. I find it very hard to sit and do nothing, as it seems like I'm wasting time, even though I know that rest is vital for wellbeing. I need to continually remind myself (or be reminded by others!) to slow down and to prioritise being instead of doing.

Don't do too much – REST

When we take on too much, we can end up feeling stressed, exhausted, overwhelmed and resentful. Many of us have a tendency to overcommit, and the reasons driving this are very different between different individuals and can vary at different stages of our lives. A useful acronym to help us gain back balance is **REST**:

Reflect: Pause and take time to reflect – consider what roles you have committed to and the impact this is having on you. Do you want to make any changes?

Explore and examine: Think about your personal reasons for being so busy. Consider what techniques might be helpful for you.

Strategies: Develop strategies for 'taking off your cape'. They could include self-questioning, affirmations, prioritisation, focusing on a process rather than an outcome, therapy, counselling, setting boundaries and working to improve self-confidence and self-acceptance.

Time to re-evaluate: Give yourself time to re-evaluate. Many people find that they make a good start on their journey of doing less, but they gradually slip back into old habits. They often only realise this when they reach the point of overwhelm again. It is important to give yourself time to re-evaluate your situation at regular intervals, to appraise whether your strategies are working and, if not, why not. Ask yourself what do you need to change to get back on track.

It is important to recognise your own warning signs that things are getting too much and that you develop your own techniques to slow down. Try and make the time and mental space for the people and things that bring you joy, and enjoy the journey rather than travel with blinkers towards your destination.

BOX 3: HOW TO ACHIEVE A SATISFACTORY WORK-LIFE BALANCE (ADAPTED FROM A PRESCRIPTION FOR HEALTHY LIVING)

- **Take time to reflect**. Life can be so busy that it can be hard to find the time to assess its reality. It is very important to pause and to take stock. If life's hope and expectations don't match current circumstances, it is important to consider what changes need to be made to get back on the desired pathway.
- **Take responsibility**. Nobody is going to tell you how to achieve your optimum work-life balance. It is something for which you need to take responsibility. Decide what your priorities are and act accordingly. A well-known saying states that: 'You will never find time for anything. If you want time, you must make it' (Charles Buxton).
- **Prioritise**. To be good at anything in life, time needs to be devoted to it. Time is finite, and it is not possible to increase the number of hours in the day. This means that you need to choose carefully how to use your time.
- **Do not take on too much**. There are some things in life that have to be done, and there is no choice in the matter. However, there are other activities, tasks, projects or events where there is a choice. Sometimes these can be fun and interesting, but if doing them means that you're putting yourself under excessive pressure, it is advisable to think twice before agreeing.
- **Work efficiently**. It can be tempting to believe that long hours need to be put in at work for efforts to be rewarded. While this may be true at times, it is not always the case. It is more important to think about the quality rather than the quantity of work. If work is performed efficiently and productively, tasks can often be completed in a shorter time than if the stage is reached when focus is lost.
- **Learn to say 'no' without feeling the need to justify your reasons**. Once other people understand the boundaries that

you have set, they are less likely to try and push you into doing things you do not want to do.

- **Leave work at work**. In the digital era, it is all too easy to bring work home. It is now common to check work emails outside of working hours and to carry on working on mobile devices. This results in the mind being continually active and never getting the opportunity to 'switch off'. As well as having an adverse impact on our sense of wellbeing, it can be harmful to relationships due to continual distraction.

One reason for preoccupation with work is because you might be worried about the jobs you need to complete the following day. In this situation, it can be helpful to write a 'to do' list and leave it at work. Once the list is written, tasks are out of your mind and on a piece of paper, which can reduce anxiety about forgetting anything.

If you work from home, it can be helpful to have designated work-free areas and work-free times of the day.

- **Forget about perfection**. Throughout life, it is usual to be encouraged to do your best and to try your hardest. While this may be necessary at certain times and for some roles, in other instances, it is absolutely fine to just get by. 'Good' can change to 'good enough'.
- **Take a break**. Many people have jobs that require self-discipline and self-direction. It is common to work solidly for hours without a break, which is not good for anyone. As well as the physical health risks associated with sedentary behaviour, you lose concentration when you work continually and your productivity falls. It is much better to take regular breaks so you don't get overwhelmed. Similarly, if you start to experience the signs of burnout, you may need to take a break from work completely to allow yourself to rest and recover before you reach crisis point.

- **Get help where you can and when you need it**. This is relevant on two levels. First, if you are feeling stressed, anxious or that you are losing control, it is advisable to seek help before the situation gets any worse. This might mean talking to a family doctor, a counsellor, an occupational health advisor, a friend or a mental health charity. Talking through difficulties can be helpful, and strategies can be explored to ease the burden. Secondly, do what you can to make life easier for yourself! This will vary according to an individual's circumstances but could include options such as online shopping or letting children have school dinners rather than packed lunches.
- **Eat well, exercise, sleep well**. Diet, activity levels and sleep all have a profound impact on wellbeing. If you concentrate on devoting a small amount of time and effort to these, you will feel more resilient when you face the challenges of life.
- **Make small changes**. Sometimes people realise that their lives are not how they had hoped or planned, and they become aware they need to make changes. These changes may be so great that they can't be achieved in a short time frame. You may want to change career or move home. If this is the case, it can be helpful to focus on small changes which can be made immediately. This will allow you to start to take control of the situation, and the impact of small changes can be huge. You might want to write your CV so that you are prepared for future job applications or declutter a room so your house is ready to be put on the market.
- **Do what you enjoy and make time for yourself**. It is all too common for people to put themselves at the bottom of their priority list. However, if you neglect to look after yourself, you will not have the emotional reserves to care for those around you or to work to the best of your abilities. It is important that you make time for the things that make you happy.
- **Get organised**. A few simple actions can have an enormous

effect on helping life to run smoothly. A practical example includes batch cooking. ·

- **Don't feel guilty**. This is one of the key aspects in achieving a work-life balance. Never feel guilty about the decisions you make! Choose the path that is right for you and have faith in your journey.
- **Be careful with technology and social media**. Digital devices offer major pros and cons in achieving a work-life balance. While they can allow more flexibility, for example, they can help you to work from home, they can also blur the line between work time and downtime. It can be useful to address how much time you spend at a screen and to think about whether this time is being spent productively and meaningfully.

Meditation and mindfulness

Practising meditation and mindfulness has a range of positive effects on our mental and physical wellbeing. These benefits are seen at a subcellular level, for example, affecting whether our genes are turned on or off, right through to a behavioural level. Our genes are like recipes – they tell our bodies which proteins to make. Not all genes are active at a given point. as we only need certain proteins at certain times. They can be thought of as being 'on' or 'off'.

Meditation describes an intentional practice during which someone will train their attention and awareness to achieve a calm state. Most people who practise meditation will specifically set aside time to do so. It is an introspective activity and is often referred to as a process of 'looking in'. There are several different schools of meditation, which differ in their underlying philosophies and the ways in which they are practised. For example, Transcendental meditation involves repeating a personal mantra, whereas Metta meditation (which is also known as Loving Kindness meditation) involves directing positive and kind thoughts towards yourself before extending them out to others and to the world.

Mindfulness is the conscious ability to be present in the given moment. It describes being fully aware of ourselves, what we are doing or what is around us. Because we might focus our attention on external objects, it can be thought of as 'looking out'. Although we can set aside time to practise mindfulness, we can also do it as part of our everyday routine activities. When cleaning our teeth, we can notice the colour and shape of the toothbrush and its bristles and we can observe how the toothpaste smells, tastes and feels against our tongue and teeth.

One of the tremendous benefits of meditation and mindfulness is that they can help us to focus. Studies have found that we spend nearly half of our time with our 'mind wandering' which means that we are thinking about things other than the task in hand. When we're having a shower, we might be planning dinner, what to get our friend for their birthday and when we need to pick up the children from school. Interestingly, mind-wandering has been shown to correlate with feelings of unhappiness. Meditation and mindfulness can help us to quieten our internal chatter, and when we are fully present in the given moment this can enhance our sense of positive wellbeing.

Meditation and mindfulness also have a wealth of other benefits. Some of these are due to the activation of our parasympathetic nervous system, which calms us down. As well as reducing stress and improving our mood, research has shown that meditation and mindfulness can reduce our blood pressure and our risk of heart disease, they have a positive impact on our immune system and they can reduce the activity of genes involved in inflammation. Meditation and mindfulness can change the way we interpret pain, reducing its severity and its 'unpleasantness', they increase the activity in the areas of our brains associated with positive mood and they even increase the amount of grey matter in brain regions involved in learning and memory, perspective taking and emotion regulation.

Many people find that meditation and mindfulness can improve relationship satisfaction and self-awareness and can foster compassion and empathy. Additional benefits are that they are free, easy to do and can be done anywhere at any time.

> **Cath, lawyer, age 42**
> *I started to practise meditation when I was suffering from anxiety. Guided practices helped me to take control of my breathing, which I found incredibly helpful in calming my busy mind and encouraging relaxation. I would choose a daily affirmation to attach to my practice – these included confidence, calmness and feelings of empowerment. I would choose an affirmation depending on what emotions I needed to turn to on a particular day.*

Are there any disadvantages to practising meditation and mindfulness?

For most people, the answer is no. Meditation and mindfulness are usually safe and effective. However, it is important to be aware that for a small number of individuals, there may be side effects such as triggering or worsening symptoms of anxiety or depression. If you experience any adverse effects, stop your practice and speak to your guide.

How do I start meditating?

I believe that we can approach meditation in a similar way to exercise. We wouldn't go from being inactive to running a marathon within a week, we would build up slowly. It can be sensible to start meditation by practising for a few minutes every day, then increasing the duration over time. Some schools of thought suggest that we should be meditating for continued stretches of forty-five minutes, but there is emerging evidence that its benefits may occur after ten to twenty minutes. It's also helpful to know that the frequency of meditation is more important than its duration, so it's far better to meditate for ten minutes on most days of the week rather than for an hour on one day.

There are lots of apps and online videos which can guide your practice, and many places have live meditation classes. Some simple exercises which you can begin at home are:

- **Focus on your breath**. Sit comfortably and notice how your body is being supported by your chair or by the floor. Draw your attention to your breathing. Notice how the air feels as it moves in and out through your nostrils. Feel the sensation as it reaches the back of your nose. Notice the movements of your chest and abdomen as they rise and fall with each breath. It's normal that thoughts will pop into your mind. When this happens, acknowledge them without judgment and bring your attention back to your breath. Continue this practice for a few minutes.
- **Balloon breathing**. When we're stressed, our breathing is often rapid and shallow. The technique of balloon breathing encourages deep and restorative breaths. Sit quietly with your eyes closed and imagine that there is a balloon in your tummy. Breathe slowly in through your nose and use each breath to fill the balloon. When you exhale, let the balloon deflate of its own accord.
- **Box breathing**. To box breathe, imagine that your breaths are following the outside of a square. Breathe in to the count of four seconds, hold your breath for four seconds, exhale for four seconds, hold for four seconds and repeat. Some people initially find the breath-holding steps can be difficult. If this happens, just pause for a couple of seconds until you get used

to the practice, then you can gradually increase the duration of the hold.

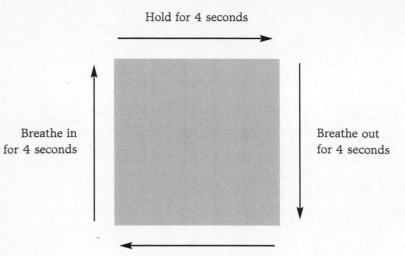

Hold for 4 seconds

Breathe in for 4 seconds

Breathe out for 4 seconds

Hold for 4 seconds

- **Body scan**. Begin your body scan by getting into a comfortable position. Close your eyes and focus on your breathing for several minutes. Now, bring your attention to your feet, noticing any sensations which are present. Hold your attention here for around thirty seconds, before releasing it and moving up your body. Travel from your feet to your calves, knees, thighs, bottom, tummy, chest, hands, arms, shoulders and face. I like to tense the muscles at each position as I move through. Hold your muscles tight for three seconds before relaxing and releasing all the tension. Once your body scan is complete, focus on your breathing before you re-engage with the world.
- **Mindful eating**. The practice of mindfulness can be applied to almost everything we do. If you eat an apple, start by noticing its shape and its colour. Is it shiny? Does it have a stalk? Note how heavy it feels in your hand and what texture its skin has. As you take a bite, be aware of the sounds as you

crunch. Did you feel your taste buds tingle? What did it smell like? How does it taste? Be aware of the muscles in your throat moving as you swallow.

Rachel, embodied growth coach and trauma-sensitive meditation and mindfulness teacher, 52

Meditation has been extremely helpful for me. It has been a safe haven when I've needed to regain composure, perspective and mental clarity, and it has led me to logical, empathetic thought when I believed that was impossible. Meditation has opened my heart to forgiveness for others and compassion for myself.

Practising meditation has helped me learn not to dwell in suffering or pain and has been important in recovering my self-worth. It has allowed me to set boundaries without guilt, to share my experiences with others and to acknowledge and release distress.

In recent years, meditation has assisted me in following my purpose in life, my soul's journey. Although my dreams and aspirations were always present, they were easy to push to one side and ignore. I tried to be the person that others thought I was or who they wanted me to be. Meditation has allowed me to be more comfortable with my true spirituality and with myself. I now have no embarrassment in showing others who I am or how I truly feel.

The practice of meditation has improved my creativity and self-confidence. I've also experienced positive 'side effects', such as making connections with others and recognising opportunities as they arise. I seize the moment. Previously, opportunities were missed, and intuition was ignored because I had 'no room' for anything else. All was rushed, work and to-do lists that never ended, fitting things in, not enjoying the occasion. So much stress. Now there is less reactivity in my behaviours, more space in my mind and I have a life which gives me room to breathe, to make the right decisions at the right time and to enjoy the process of simply being. I no longer have the need to fit this square into a round hole. I've reconnected to me.

Gratitude

Being grateful is good for our wellbeing. It encourages us to recognise the good in the world, which boosts our mood and feelings of being content. Practising gratitude helps us to face life's challenges with determination and resilience.

Dr Sonal Shah, a GP and lifestyle medicine doctor, explains why gratitude is so beneficial for us:

The practice of gratitude is a simple and effective way of combating negative emotions by reminding us of what is good in our lives. It encourages us to put things in perspective and trains our mind to focus on the things we are thankful for. There is evidence that gratitude can improve our emotional state, our social wellbeing, our health and even our career. Studies have reported that people who practise gratitude are happier, report fewer health complaints and spend more time exercising. They may be more enthusiastic, determined, attentive and have more energy, and are they are less likely to be depressed, anxious or lonely.

Gratitude motivates people to make positive changes in their lives and in the world around them. Some easy ways to practise gratitude are:

- **Five good things.** *Sit quietly for five minutes and think about five things that you're grateful for. Try and be as specific as possible, for example, 'I am grateful I am fit enough to cycle to work'.*
- **Gratitude journal.** *Writing a short daily journal entry about positive experiences encourages reflection and clarity of thinking.*
- **Writing a letter of thanks.** *Hand-writing letters is a skill that is sadly being lost in the digital era. When we say thank you to*

someone this is not just beneficial for ourselves. It brings happiness to others and strengthens relationships.

- **Gratitude jar.** *Make a note of your positive experiences and put these in a jar. If you're feeling down, reading one of these notes may help to improve your mood.*
- **Be mindful of the language we use.** *Our words and thoughts can have a large impact on our mood and emotions. A commonly cited example is that if we say, 'I get to make the packed lunches/ unload the dishwasher/ hoover etc' rather than 'I have to...' this can alter the way we think about and approach our day-to-day lives.*

Toxic positivity

Although fostering a positive mindset has many benefits for our wellbeing, it is important to be aware that there are many situations that we can't view in a positive light. If we always try to find the good in everything, there is a danger that we won't permit and process negative emotions, which are a part of the human experience. It is important that we allow ourselves to feel sad, angry, lonely, low and that we seek help and support when we need it.

Kindness

'In a world where you can be anything, be kind.'
Jennifer Dukes Lee

Kindness is all around us. Sometimes we just need to make the effort to look for it. More importantly, we should all make a conscious endeavour to be kind. To other people, to ourselves and to the world. Being kind is good for us. Acts of kindness are associated with the release of the 'love hormone' oxytocin, which plays a role in bonding and social relationships.

For many people, life is hard. There is a widening gap between the rich and the poor in the UK, a quarter of the adult population will experience a mental health problem each year and statistics show that rates of loneliness have significantly increased over the last decade. Despite the widespread use of the internet and social media, which theoretically enhances connectivity around the world, levels of community cohesion are low, and one in eight adults describe themselves as having no close friends.

Work is often a source of stress and unhappiness, and the World Health Organisation now recognises burnout as an 'occupational phenomenon' characterised by feelings of exhaustion, negativity, cynicism and reduced efficacy. Modern life places many demands on our time, and it can be difficult to juggle all our commitments, creating feelings of stress and anxiety.

What the world needs now, more than ever, is for people to be kind. To show each other compassion and warmth. To bring joy to others, to do what benefits society and promotes the best interests of all around us. When we are kind to other people, it has a positive effect on our own wellbeing and increases our own sense of happiness.

What is kindness?

There are many different definitions of kindness. *The Cambridge Dictionary* describes it as 'the quality of being generous, helpful and caring about other people, or an act showing this quality'. According to the Macmillan Dictionary, the word is derived from the old English word *kyndes* and the Middle English word *kindenes* and has its origins in 'nation, produce, increase, noble deeds, courtesy'. The great Greek philosopher Aristotle wrote that kindness is 'helpfulness towards someone in need, not in return for anything, nor for the advantage of the helper himself, but for that of the person helped'. Kindness is at the core of most of the world's religions.

In its simplest form, *kindness is characterised by behaviours that are performed in a selfless manner to improve the wellbeing of others and of the world.*

Some scientists believe it was kindness that primed the human species for language development. When early humans started to prefer cooperative friends and mates to aggressive ones, they started to become 'tamer'. This was associated with the evolution of a variety of physical and biochemical characteristics which were essential for language formation.

Kindness can be recognised by babies as young as six months old. Research has shown that infants take into consideration an individual's actions towards others in evaluating that individual as appealing or aversive. Babies prefer people who help others compared to those who hinder others or are neutral. This capacity may play a role in forming the foundations of moral behaviours.

Being kind is good for you

Acts of kindness benefit everyone – the 'giver', the 'receiver' and society as a whole. Research has shown that the performance of selfless acts may have positive health benefits. A study looking at nearly two thousand adults found that those who take part in voluntary activities had lower levels of C-Reactive Protein (CRP) in their blood. CRP is an indicator of inflammation and is associated with chronic diseases such as high blood pressure, stroke and heart disease. Volunteering has also been linked to positive wellbeing, reduced symptoms of depression, improved self-ratings of health and better control of blood pressure.

The significant and positive effects of kindness can impact many domains of life: practising kindness has been found to reduce social anxiety, it is associated with respect from others and may even reduce the severity and duration of the common cold.

Kindness also has a role to play in spending habits and wellbeing. Both children and adults who purchase goods for others, or give treats away, experience greater happiness than when they receive products themselves, illustrating the hedonic benefits of generosity.

While self-care and self-kindness are fundamental components of wellbeing, interestingly, it has been shown that prosocial or kind behaviours towards others result in greater increases in psychological flourishing than do self-focused behaviours, meaning that to boost mood it is important for people to treat others well.

In the healthcare system, kindness has been described as 'an essential ingredient ... because the emotion experienced by individuals when giving or receiving kindness can provide the necessary courage to take action'. Kindness is associated with increased levels of the 'feel good' chemical dopamine, which plays a role in the experience of .pleasure, reward and in motivation.

Implementing kindness: the ripple effect

Some people seem to have an inherent desire and ability to be kind to others; it comes as second nature without conscious thought. This is likely the result of a complex relationship between their genetics, the social environment they grew up in and their current life situation. For other people, kindness isn't an innate part of their being and it takes effort to perform kind behaviours. Kind acts do not need to be big, complicated or extravagant. It is often the 'small' behaviours that can make a difference to someone else. For those who are not 'naturally kind' people, it can be helpful to begin with simple acts such as offering to make someone a cup of tea, holding a door open, checking in on a friend or just letting someone know that you appreciate them.

The wonderful thing about kindness is that it has a 'ripple effect' – the recipient of a kind act is likely to 'pass it on', so the spread of warmth and positive wellbeing is enhanced. Research has shown that individuals who receive acts of kindness experience higher levels of happiness than controls, and that they are nearly three times more likely to engage in prosocial acts than others. It is clear that both givers and receivers benefit from kindness, and the effects may be long-lived. One study found that following a kindness intervention, there are short-term improvements in wellbeing, for example, in parameters such as autonomy and competence, but even two months after the intervention has ended, receivers still continue to experience happiness and givers may be less depressed and more satisfied with their jobs and their lives. Practising kindness is emotionally reinforcing and contagious.

In addition to practising kindness towards others, it is important to recognise, acknowledge and to be grateful when you receive acts of kindness. It is all too easy to take kind acts for granted, but reflection on, and appreciation of, kindness can further increase psychological wellbeing and emotional resilience.

'Be kind whenever possible. It is always possible.'
The 14th Dalai Lama

Sleep

Dr Emma Short

Exercise and movement are the lifestyle interventions I enjoy the most, but sleep is the one I will always prioritise. When I get enough sleep, I feel energetic, motivated and focused. When I am tired, I am grumpy and irritable. I tend to eat rubbish, I find it harder to exercise and I often experience a low mood.

In this chapter, we'll look at what happens as we sleep and why a decent night's rest is so important for our wellbeing.

What is sleep?

Without a doubt, sleep is an absolute requirement for our health and wellbeing, but many people fail to give it the attention it deserves. The amount of sleep we need varies between different people and depends on our age, but most adults should aim for around eight hours a night.

All of us have an internal 'body clock' which usually has a twenty-four-hour, or 'circadian', rhythm. This rhythm is incredibly important. It ensures that the systems within our bodies can carry out their functions at the correct time. For example, at night we produce higher levels of a hormone called anti-diuretic hormone (ADH) than we do during the day. ADH reduces the amount of urine we produce so we don't need to keep going to the loo when we should be sleeping. In humans, a hormone called leptin also peaks at night. Leptin acts as an appetite suppressant so helps to stop us eating when we're in bed. When we wake up, we produce the stress hormone cortisol to help us deal with the day ahead. Sleep is a vital part of this daily rhythm.

Our circadian cycle is under the control of a tiny part of our brain called the suprachiasmatic nucleus (SCN). This is largely regulated by the amount of light it receives. When it's bright, the SCN knows it's daytime, so it tells us to stay alert and awake. As the evening draws in, and darkness falls, the SCN initiates the production of the 'sleepy hormone' melatonin, which promotes sleep. Melatonin works hand in hand with a chemical called adenosine. During waking hours, there is a build-up of adenosine in our brains. When this reaches a certain level, it acts as a trigger to make us feel drowsy and tired.

Once we actually fall asleep, we go through several sleep cycles each night. Each cycle lasts around ninety minutes, but the duration increases as the night goes on. The cycles are composed of four parts, although this can be simplified into Rapid Eye Movement (REM) sleep and Non-REM sleep:

- REM sleep: REM sleep usually lasts between ten minutes and an hour. During REM sleep, our bodies are temporarily paralysed, but our eyes are moving rapidly behind our eyelids. It is during REM sleep that we dream, and REM sleep is essential for brain functions such as consolidating memories.

- Non-REM sleep has three parts. During this time, everything slows down – our heart rate, breathing rate and brain activity all reduce. Non-REM sleep is vital for growth and repair. It is also important for the functioning of our immune systems and forming memories.

Many important physiological functions happen as we sleep. As well as the hormones mentioned above, we also produce growth hormone at night. Growth hormone is important for growth in children and adolescents. In adults, it is involved in regulating our body composition and metabolism. When we are asleep, our muscles are repaired, and there are changes in our immune system. At night, we also get rid of toxic waste products from our brains.

What happens if we don't get enough sleep?

I'm sure most of us know how we feel when we are tired … moody, short-tempered and we may find it harder than usual to concentrate! However, the impact of poor sleep doesn't stop there. When we're sleep deficient, we might have difficulties solving problems, making decisions and regulating our emotions. Research has found that chronic sleep deprivation increases our risk of high blood pressure, type 2 diabetes, heart disease and stroke. We're more likely to gain weight and develop obesity, to pick up infections and to suffer from depression. Many of these effects are seen because of the hormonal dysregulation that occurs when we don't get enough shut-eye.

Sleeping difficulties

A lot of people describe having sleeping difficulties. For some, this can be a one-night only event, but for others, sleeping problems can become long term. This can have a profound impact on wellbeing and quality of life. Statistics show that over a third of UK adults find it hard to get to sleep at least once a week, and one in five people have trouble falling asleep every single night. Generally, women have more sleep difficulties than men, and the age group most commonly affected is those aged between forty-five to fifty-four years.

Sleeping problems come in different guises – some people find it hard to drop off, others wake frequently at night, some people wake early in the morning and others feel unrefreshed after sleep. There are several medical conditions that are associated with sleeping difficulties, including depression, anxiety, schizophrenia, any cause of pain and hyperthyroidism. Certain medications can also impact sleep, such as some steroids and certain treatments for high blood pressure. We can also have problems with sleep if our circadian rhythm is out of kilter, for example, if we work shifts. However, for a lot of people, stress is a major player in causing insomnia.

Amy, receptionist, age 33

I have had insomnia for as long as I can remember. I get nights where my brain will just not switch off. It's as though I can't stop thinking about every little thing I've said or done that day, or what I need to do the next day. It doesn't matter how tired I am, when night comes, I just can't sleep. I have a four-month-old baby now, so my sleep is even more interrupted. People tell me to 'sleep when the baby sleeps' but even when she is asleep, I can't drop off. I am a very light sleeper which doesn't help, as the slightest noise wakes me.

When I don't get enough sleep, I feel really down, and it also affects me physically. I suffer from fibromyalgia, and a lack of sleep makes my joint pain flare up.

I have tried all sorts of strategies to try and improve my sleep: tablets, sleep meditation apps, calm music and lavender sprays, but none of these work for me. Sometimes a hot bath before bed can have a positive effect, and when I am feeling mentally rested my sleep improves. My sleep is best when I am on holiday by the sea.

Joyce, retired, age 92

I am usually in bed by 9.30 pm. Normally, I fall asleep after around half an hour, and I generally sleep until I need a toilet visit in the early hours of the morning. It is at this time that I find it hard to get back to sleep. Worries often pop up in my mind. I try to distract myself or do breathing exercises, which sometimes help but not always. If I manage to nod back off, I usually wake up just after 5 am, and I lie in bed until 7.30 am. Occasionally I can't sleep when I first go to bed, and I am still awake in the early hours of the morning. When this happens, I am very restless for the whole of the night.

If I haven't slept well, I feel tired the next day, but I always manage to get through the day without falling asleep. I put my poor sleep down to 'old age'. I am 92 and I always slept well when I was much younger.

How to improve our sleeping habits

Some individuals experience such significant problems with sleep that they need input from a healthcare professional. This is especially important if the sleeping difficulties are related to an underlying health problem or medications, or if an individual might benefit from cognitive behavioural therapy (CBT). However, there are many actions that we can take at home to improve our sleep:

- **Reduce caffeine intake and limit it to the morning**. One of our internal sleeping cues is the rising levels of adenosine that accumulate in our brains during the day. Caffeine has several effects on our bodies, one of which is that it blocks the receptors that adenosine acts on. This means that adenosine can't activate our feelings of being drowsy. If you're having problems sleeping, it's sensible to cut down your caffeine intake and to avoid any caffeine-containing drinks or foods after lunchtime.
- **Avoid alcohol**. Although alcohol can help us to fall asleep, it reduces the quality and duration of sleep. Alcohol also acts as a diuretic, so can wake us at night as it makes us need to pass urine.
- **Don't smoke**. Smoking has many harmful effects, which include a negative impact on our sleep. Smoking is associated with

difficulties initiating sleep, and it also affects the quality of sleep, causing smokers to spend less time in deeper sleep states. Smokers have an overall shorter sleep duration than non-smokers, and their sleep is more fragmented. Most of these effects are due to the stimulant effects of nicotine and because smokers effectively experience smoking withdrawal at night.

- **Don't eat too late**. If our stomachs are full when we go to bed, this can make it harder to sleep. In addition to this, lying flat increases the risk of reflux.
- **Exercise and spend time outside**. As well as reducing stress levels, exercise tires us out and has been shown to significantly improve our sleep. It's best if vigorous activities are not done too close to bedtime, and we should aim to be active outside during the sunlight hours, as this reinforces our circadian rhythm.
- **Don't drink too much in the evening**. You don't want your sleep to be disturbed by trips to the toilet.
- **Watch when you nap**. If you nap during the day, try to keep it to a maximum of twenty minutes duration, and nap as early as possible. Late afternoon naps often delay the onset of night-time sleep, as our body clocks can get confused about whether it's daytime or night-time.
- **Listen to your body**. If you start to feel sleepy in the evening, listen to the messages your body is sending you. Even if it seems earlier than usual, head to bed once you are drowsy.
- **Wind down during the hour before you go to bed**. Aim to slow down as bedtime gets closer. You could dim the lights and do an activity you find relaxing, such as having a bath, listening to music or reading a book.
- **Avoid digital devices**. As described previously in this book, our digital devices have the potential to adversely affect our sleep in several ways. The blue light they emit can impair the production of melatonin, and when we're active on social media this can keep our minds active. Try and digitally disconnect for the two to three hours before you want to sleep.

- **Stress reduction.** Stress is a major cause of sleeping problems, and it's incredibly helpful if the underlying cause of stress can be dealt with. Many of the lifestyle interventions described throughout this book are also useful tools in stress management, including meditation, mindfulness and physical activity.
- **Optimise your sleeping environment.** Try and make your bedroom as sleep friendly as possible. This involves trying to keep it dark, cool and quiet. Ensure your bed is comfortable. Remove all digital devices and only use the bed for sleeping or intimate activities.
- **Go to bed and wake up at a consistent time every day.** To try and help your body to have a consistent circadian rhythm, it is important that you go to bed and get up at the same time every day – unfortunately this means no weekend lie-ins!
- **Consider lavender.** Although the evidence isn't definitive, some studies have found that lavender oil may have a small to moderate effect in improving sleep. *I personally like to use a lavender mist on my pillow at night.*

One of the issues with sleeping difficulties is that they can soon create a vicious circle – often when we can't sleep, we become worried or anxious about it, and this then exacerbates the sleep problems and the cycle continues. If you find you're lying in bed awake at night, give yourself around twenty minutes to fall back to sleep. If you're still awake after this time, consider getting out of bed, keeping the environment dark and quiet. Carry out a calming, low impact activity which doesn't require much brain power, such as stretching, yoga or doing some ironing. It's usually sensible to stay out of the bedroom for thirty to sixty minutes, then return and try to get back to sleep.

I am fortunate in that I usually sleep quite well, but I can appreciate the impact that poor sleep has on people. If I ever wake at night and can't drop off again, I get increasingly anxious. I watch the clock and continually calculate the number of hours sleep I will end up having. I worry about how I will feel the next day and get frustrated that I am awake.

Some people may need additional help and support with their sleeping. Cognitive behavioural therapy (CBT) is a recognised therapy for insomnia (CBTi) and is based on the principle that our thoughts, feelings and behaviours are all interrelated. During CBT for insomnia, a therapist may address how any negative thoughts and feelings are affecting sleep, and they might explore any behaviours that are not conducive to sleep. Some of the techniques used during CBTi include sleep restriction therapy, remaining passively awake and relaxation. Sleep restriction therapy involves trying to maximise sleep efficiency – ensuring that the time we spend in bed is time actually asleep. During sleep restriction, individuals stay awake as long as possible so that when they do go to bed, they are too tired not to sleep. Over time, they gradually go to bed earlier, with the aim that slowly the sleep-wake cycle will be reset. Remaining passively awake, which is also known as 'paradoxical intention' encompasses avoiding efforts to fall asleep. The goal is to avoid 'performance anxiety' about sleep – we try to stay awake so that the act of 'falling asleep' doesn't become an event associated with stress and anxiety.

It is important to be aware that any of these interventions should only be considered after a discussion with a qualified therapist, as they may not suit everyone, and may actually be contraindicated for some people as they could do more harm than good.

To summarise, sleep is a biological necessity, which is just as important as eating and drinking. We often push sleep to the bottom of our 'to do' list, but it should be there at the top. When we are well rested, we feel happier and more energetic, our performance is enhanced and we are more likely to make healthier life choices.

Empowerment

Throughout this book, we've described many different lifestyle changes which could help you to feel healthier, happier and energised. But, if you want to make a change for the better, you need to feel you have the power to do it.

Being empowered means that you have control over your life and your choices. There are several factors which contribute to being empowered. These include knowledge, confidence, self-esteem, ability, support networks, resilience, motivation and commitment. For example, if you want to change your diet so you increase the diversity of your gut microbiome, you would need:

- **Knowledge**. You need to know what the gut microbiome is and what foods have an impact on its composition.
- **Confidence and self-esteem**. It is important for you to believe in yourself and in your ability to put your plans into action.
- **Ability**. You need to be able to buy the appropriate foods and to cook suitable meals.
- **Support networks**. Support networks are powerful. Never underestimate the strength of your support crew. If you surround yourselves with like-minded people, the behaviour you are trying to adopt is often seen as the 'norm', which makes it easier for it to become a habit. If the only foods your friends and family offer you are high in fibre, you will be working towards your goal with minimal effort on your part. On the other hand, if your friends are dismissive of what you are trying to achieve and try to persuade you to eat lots of processed foods, you are more likely to lose motivation and will need considerable willpower to stick to your plans.

- **Resilience**. You need to be able to cope with the challenges that you encounter in life. On your journey to good health, these may come in several forms, for example, suffering an injury when you are trying to get fit, not losing weight at the rate you would like or having an argument with someone you care about. There are several ways that you can enhance your personal resilience, and these can be helpful in giving you the strength to pick yourself back up if you fall. Strategies include:
  - **Acceptance**. When things go wrong, or when you come across hurdles in your path, it can be easy to feel resentful that life isn't a smooth journey or to look for someone or something to blame. It is important to accept that hiccups are inevitable, and they often can't be predicted or prevented. Rather than fight against them, accept they are part of life. It's how you deal with them that matters.
  - **Take control**. Difficult encounters or situations can cause you to react without thought. This can be a 'gut response' driven by your subconscious mind or your emotions. For example, if a child was about to run into the road, you would grab them to keep them safe. In this case, the immediate reaction is a necessity. However, a tendency to instantly react is not always beneficial: if you are criticised, it might not be in your best interests to argue back. It is helpful to learn how to *respond* instead. When something happens to upset or trigger you, take a moment to pause. Notice the feelings and sensations you are experiencing and consider how you want to behave. This can help you to take back control of a situation and can encourage a more favourable outcome.
  - **Take action**. When you are in a tricky or undesirable situation, consider what you could do to improve things. Try not to dwell; rather, take proactive steps to get you back on track. If you have a knee injury through running, you could go for a swim instead; if you notice that your eating habits have started to become less healthy, fill your fridge with vegetables and shut away the biscuits.

- **Learn from experience.** Reflect on any previous challenges you have faced – think about the techniques and strategies which worked for you. Assess whether these could be useful in your current situation.
- **Look for the good, but allow yourself to process any difficult emotions.** Frequently when things don't go as planned, you can focus on the negative. Whilst it is vital that you allow yourself the time and space to process any difficult emotions, in many situations you can look for the good. This can help in developing a growth mindset, and you can learn from your mistakes and from the challenges you have faced. Praise yourself when something has gone well.
- **See the bigger picture.** Sometimes, when facing adversity, you can become slightly blinkered. Thoughts and headspace become funnelled down on to the issue in hand. It is really helpful to take a step back and to see the bigger picture. To appreciate that everything occurs in a context. Remind yourself of what you have already achieved and how far you have come.

- **Motivation and commitment.** When we want to make healthy changes, we must be sufficiently motivated to do so. Motivation is like a force – it's what drives you to take action, then it keeps you committed. Your motivation levels can be affected by many factors, including your thoughts, feelings, desires and emotional state. But physical factors also play a part, such as whether you're tired or hungry. If you're thinking about setting a health-related goal, be honest with yourself about how motivated you really are to achieve it. I speak to a lot of people who want to lose weight, but when they really question themselves, they find that, deep down, they're not actually motivated to commit to the changes they need to make. Motivation can be ranked on a scale of one to ten. If you want to change your behaviours, you really need at least a seven in motivation levels to be successful.

If you're trying to change your lifestyle, this can be a helpful checklist to run through. Ask yourself – *do I have the knowledge I need? Do I believe in myself and my abilities? Do I have people around who will support me? Am I really motivated to do this?* If you find that you're answering 'no' to any of these, explore the ways in which you could change this to a 'yes'.

If I can help in any way, please get in touch. I'd love to hear from you and to support you on your wellbeing journey.

My Prescription for You

I hope you've enjoyed reading this book and that you've got some ideas about changes you'd like to make to energise your life.

My prescription for you is to ...

- move your body in a way you love
- surround yourself with people who light up your soul
- prioritise sleep
- be grateful and look for the good
- give yourself the time and space to process difficult emotions
- spend time in nature
- nourish your body and mind
- rest
- be kind

References

Welcome

Short Emma (ed.). *A Prescription for Healthy Living: A Guide to Lifestyle Medicine*. Elsevier; 2021.

Diaz KM, Howard VJ et al. Patterns of Sedentary Behaviour and Mortality in US Middle-Aged and Older Adults. A National Cohort Study. *Annals of Internal Medicine*. 2017. 167(7): 465–475

www.who.int/health-topics/cancer

https://www.euro.who.int/en/health-topics/noncommunicable-diseases/cardiovascular-diseases/data-and-statistics

Exercise and Movement

Argilés JM, Campos N, Lopez-Pedrosa JM, Rueda R, Rodriguez-Mañas L. Skeletal Muscle Regulates Metabolism via Interorgan Crosstalk: Roles in Health and Disease. *J Am Med Dir Assoc*. 2016 Sep 1;17(9):789–96.

Bailey DP. Editorial: sedentary behavior in human health and disease. *Front Physiol*. 2017. https://doi.org/10.3389/fphys.2017.00901.

Biswas A, Oh PI, Faulkner GE, Bajaj RR, Silver MA, Mitchell MS, Alter DA. Sedentary time and its association with risk for disease incidence, mortality, and hospitalization in adults: a systematic review and meta-analysis. *Ann Intern Med*. 2015 Jan 20;162(2):123–32. doi: 10.7326/M14-1651. Erratum in: Ann Intern Med. 2015 Sep 1;163(5):400. PMID: 25599350.

Carlson SA, Fulton JE, Schoenborn CA, Loustalot F. Trend and prevalence estimates based on the 2008 Physical Activity Guidelines for Americans. *Am J Prev Med*. 2010 Oct;39(4):305–13.

Daly RM, Dalla Via J, Duckham RL, Fraser SF, Helge EW. Exercise for the prevention of osteoporosis in postmenopausal women: an evidence-based guide to the optimal prescription. *Braz J Phys Ther*. 2019 Mar–Apr;23(2):170–180.

Diaz KM, Howard VJ, Hutto B, Colabianchi N, Vena JE, Safford MM, Blair SN, Hooker SP. Patterns of Sedentary Behavior and Mortality in U.S. Middle-Aged and Older Adults: A National Cohort Study. *Ann Intern Med*. 2017 Oct 3;167(7):465–475.

Dimeo F, Bauer M, Varahram I, Proest G, Halter U. Benefits from aerobic exercise in patients with major depression: a pilot study. *Br J Sports Med*. 2001 Apr;35(2):114–7.

Ekelund U, Steene-Johannessen J, Brown WJ, Fagerland MW, Owen N, Powell KE, Bauman A, Lee IM; Lancet Physical Activity Series 2 Executive Committee; Lancet Sedentary Behaviour Working Group. Does physical activity attenuate, or even eliminate, the detrimental association of sitting time with mortality? A harmonised meta-analysis of data from more than 1 million men and women. *Lancet*. 2016 Sep 24;388(10051):1302–10.

Falck RS, Landry GJ, Best JR, Davis JC, Chiu BK, Liu-Ambrose T. Cross-Sectional Relationships of Physical Activity and Sedentary Behavior With Cognitive Function in Older Adults With Probable Mild Cognitive Impairment. *Phys Ther*. 2017 Oct 1;97(10):975–984.

Franklin BA, Swain DP, Shephard RJ. New insights in the prescription of exercise for coronary patients. *J Cardiovasc Nurs*. 2003;18:116–23.

Fulton JE, Garg M, Galuska DA, Rattay KT, Caspersen CJ. Public health and clinical recommendations for physical activity and physical fitness: special focus on overweight youth. *Sports Med*. 2004;34(9):581–99.

Ghadieh AS, Saab B. Evidence for exercise training in the management of hypertension in adults. *Can Fam Physician*. 2015;61(3):233–239.

Gómez-Bruton A, Matute-Llorente Á, González-Agüero A, Casajús JA,

Vicente-Rodríguez G. Plyometric exercise and bone health in children and adolescents: a systematic review. *World J Pediatr*. 2017 Apr;13(2):112–121.

Guitar NA. The effects of physical exercise on executive function in community-dwelling older adults living with Alzheimer's type dementia: a systematic review. *Ageing Research Reviews 2018;* 47: 159–167.

https://assets.publishing.service.gov.uk/government/uploads/system/uploads/attachment_data/file/213740/dh_128145.pdf.

https://www.gov.uk/government/collections/physical-activity-guidelines.

https://edition.cnn.com/2017/09/11/health/sitting-increases-risk-of-death-study/index.html.

Hambrecht R, Niebauer J, Marburger C, Grunze M, Kälberer B, Hauer K, Schlierf G, Kübler W, Schuler G. Various intensities of leisure time physical activity in patients with coronary artery disease: effects on cardiorespiratory fitness and progression of coronary atherosclerotic lesions. *J Am Coll Cardiol*. 1993 Aug;22(2):468–77.

Heath R. Sitting Ducks, sedentary behaviour and its health risks: part one of a two-part series *BSJM blog series*. 2015. https://blogs.bmj.com/bjsm/2015/01/21/sitting-ducks-sedentary-behaviour-and-its-healthrisks-part-one-of-a-two-part-series/.

Iacobucci G. Sedentary lifestyle is putting middle ages health at risk, PHE warns. *BMJ*. 2017;358:j3995.

Ibrahim EM, Al-Homaidh A. Physical activity and survival after breast cancer diagnosis: meta-analysis of published studies. *Med Oncol*. 2011 Sep;28(3):753–65.

Keating SE, Johnson NA, Mielke GI, Coombes JS. A systematic review and meta-analysis of interval training versus moderate-intensity continuous training on body adiposity. *Obes Rev*. 2017 Aug;18(8):943–964.

Knudson DV, Magnusson P, Malachy M. Current issues in flexibility fitness. *President's Council on Physical Fitness and Sports Digest 2000*; 10: 2–10.

Laursen P and Jenkins G. The Scientific Basis for High Intensity Interval Training. *Sports Med.* 2002 32(1): 53–73.

Mason JE, Faller YN, LeBouthillier DM, Asmundson GJG. Exercise anxiety: A qualitative analysis of the barriers, facilitators, and psychological processes underlying exercise participation for people with anxiety-related disorders. *Mental Health and Physical Activity*. 2019 16:128–139.

Meyerhardt JA, Giovannucci EL, Holmes MD, Chan AT, Chan JA, Colditz GA, Fuchs CS. Physical activity and survival after colorectal cancer diagnosis. *J Clin Oncol.* 2006 Aug 1;24(22):3527–34.

Morris JN, Heady JA, Raffle PA, Roberts CG, Parks JW. Coronary heart-disease and physical activity of work. *Lancet.* 1953 Nov 21;262(6795):1053–1057.

National Health Service. Get running with couch to 5k. www.nhs.uk/live-well/exercise/get-running-with-couch-to-5k/ (accessed July 2021).

O'Donoghue, G., Perchoux, C., Mensah, K. *et al.* A systematic review of correlates of sedentary behaviour in adults aged 18–65 years: a socio-ecological approach. *BMC Public Health* 16, 163 (2016).

Owen N, Sparling PB, Healy GN, Dunstan DW, Matthews CE. Sedentary behavior: emerging evidence for a new health risk. *Mayo Clin Proc.* 2010;85(12):1138–1141.

Roy M, Williams SM, Brown RC, Meredith-Jones KA, Osborne H, Jospe M, Taylor RW. High-Intensity Interval Training in the Real World: Outcomes from a 12-Month Intervention in Overweight Adults. *Med Sci Sports Exerc.* 2018 Sep;50(9):1818–1826.

Sardinha LB, Magalhães JP, Santos DA, Júdice PB. Sedentary Patterns, Physical Activity, and Cardiorespiratory Fitness in Association to

Glycemic Control in Type 2 Diabetes Patients. *Front Physiol*. 2017 Apr 28;8:262.

Shiraev T and Barclay G. Evidence-Based Exercise. *Aus Fam Physician*. 2012 41(12): 960–962.

van der Velde JHPM, Savelberg HHCM, van der Berg JD, Sep SJS, van der Kallen CJH, Dagnelie PC, Schram MT, Henry RMA, Reijven PLM, van Geel TACM, Stehouwer CDA, Koster A, Schaper NC. Sedentary Behavior Is Only Marginally Associated with Physical Function in Adults Aged 40–75 Years – the Maastricht Study. *Front Physiol*. 2017 Apr 25;8:242.

Virtuoso Júnior JS, Roza LB, Tribess S, Meneguci J, Mendes EL, Pegorari MS, Dias FA, Dos Santos Tavares DM, Sasaki JE. Time Spent Sitting Is Associated with Changes in Biomarkers of Frailty in Hospitalized Older Adults: A Cross-Sectional Study. *Front Physiol*. 2017 Jul 31;8:505.

Warburton DE, Nicol CW, Bredin SS. Health benefits of physical activity: the evidence. *CMAJ*. 2006 Mar 14;174(6):801–9.

Weston KS, Wisløff U, Coombes JS. High-intensity interval training in patients with lifestyle-induced cardiometabolic disease: a systematic review and meta-analysis. *Br J Sports Med*. 2014 Aug;48(16):1227–34.

Wilmot EG, Edwardson CL, Achana FA, Davies MJ, Gorely T, Gray LJ, Khunti K, Yates T, Biddle SJ. Sedentary time in adults and the association with diabetes, cardiovascular disease and death: systematic review and meta-analysis. *Diabetologia*. 2012 Nov;55(11):2895–905. doi: 10.1007/s00125-012-2677-z. Epub 2012 Aug 14. Erratum in: *Diabetologia*. 2013 Apr;56(4):942–3.

https://www.health.gov.au/resources/collections/collection-of-physical-activity-and-sedentary-behaviour-guidelines-for-all-ages

Yang L, Cao C, Kantor ED, Nguyen LH, Zheng X, Park Y, Giovannucci EL, Matthews CE, Colditz GA, Cao Y. Trends in Sedentary Behavior

Among the US Population, 2001-2016. *JAMA*. 2019 Apr 23;321(16):1587–1597.

Young DR, Hivert MF, Alhassan S, Camhi SM, Ferguson JF, Katzmarzyk PT, Lewis CE, Owen N, Perry CK, Siddique J, Yong CM; Physical Activity Committee of the Council on Lifestyle and Cardiometabolic Health; Council on Clinical Cardiology; Council on Epidemiology and Prevention; Council on Functional Genomics and Translational Biology; and Stroke Council. Sedentary Behavior and Cardiovascular Morbidity and Mortality: A Science Advisory From the American Heart Association. *Circulation*. 2016 Sep 27;134(13):e262–79.

Nutrition

Short Emma (ed.). *A Prescription for Healthy Living: A Guide to Lifestyle Medicine*. Elsevier; 2021.

Alissa EM, Ferns GA. Dietary fruits and vegetables and cardiovascular diseases risk. *Crit Rev Food Sci Nutr*. 2017 Jun 13;57(9):1950–1962.

Arora T, Sharma R, Frost G. Propionate. Anti-obesity and satiety enhancing factor? *Appetite*. 2011;56(2):511–5.

Backhed F, Ley RE, Sonnenburg JL, Peterson DA, Gordon JI. Host-bacterial Mutualism in the Human Intestine. *Science*. 2005;307(5717):1915–1920.

Bajaj, J.S. Alcohol, liver disease and the gut microbiota. *Nat Rev Gastroenterol Hepatol*. 2019;16:235–246.

Butler MI, Mörkl S, Sandhu KV, Cryan JF, Dinan TG. The Gut Microbiome and Mental Health: What Should We Tell Our Patients?: Le microbiote Intestinal et la Santé Mentale : que Devrions-Nous dire à nos Patients? *Can J Psychiatry*. 2019;64(11):747–760.

de Cabo R, Mattson MP. Effects of Intermittent Fasting on Health, Aging, and Disease. *N Engl J Med*. 2019 Dec 26;381(26):2541–

2551. Erratum in: *N Engl J Med*. 2020 Jan 16;382(3):298. Erratum in: *N Engl J Med*. 2020 Mar 5;382(10):978.

Derrien M, Johan ET, Van Hylckama V. Fate, Activity and Impact of Ingested Bacteria within the Human Gut Microbiota. *Trends in Microbiology*. 2015;23(6):354–366.

Engen PA, Green SJ, Voigt RM, Forsyth CB, Keshavarzian A. The Gastrointestinal Microbiome: Alcohol Effects on the Composition of Intestinal Microbiota. *Alcohol Res*. 2015;37(2):223–36.

Ferranti EP, Dunbar SB, Dunlop AL, Corwin EJ. 20 Things You Didn't Know about the Human Gut Microbiome. *J Cardiovasc Nurs*. 2014;29(6):479–481.

Firth J, Gangwisch JE, Borsini A, Wootton RE, Mayer EA. Food and Mood: How do Diet and Nutrition affect Mental Wellbeing? *BMJ*. 2020; 369: m2382.

Flint HJ. The Impact of Nutrition on the Human Microbiome. *Nutrition Reviews*. 2012;70(suppl_1, 1):S10–S13.

Hall KD, Ayuketah A, Brychta R, Cai H, Cassimatis T, Chen KY, Chug ST, Costa E, Courville A, Darcey V, Fletcher LA, Forde CG, Gharib AM, Gua J, Howard R, Joseph PV, McGehee S, Ouwerkerk S, Raisinger K, Rozga I, Stagliano M, Walter M, Walter PJ, Yang S, Zhou M. Ultra-processed Diets Cause Excess Calorie Intake and Weight Gain: An Inpatient Randomized Controlled Trial of *Ad Libitum* Food Intake. *Cell Metab*. 2019;11:67–77.E3

Hill C, Guarner F, Reid G, Gibson GR, Merenstein DJ, Pot B, Morelli L, Canani RB, Flint HJ, Salminen S, Calder PC, Sanders ME. The International Scientific Association for Probiotics and Prebiotics Consensus Statement on the Scope and Appropriate Use of the Term Probiotic. *Nat Rev Gastroenterol Hepatol*. 2014; 11: 506–514.

Myhrstad MCW, Tunsjø H, Charnock C, Telle-Hansen VH. Dietary Fiber, Gut Microbiota, and Metabolic Regulation-Current Status in Human Randomized Trials. *Nutrients*. 2020;12(3):859.

http://healthsurvey.hscic.gov.uk/data-visualisation/data-visualisation/explore-the-trends/fruit-vegetables.aspx

https://publichealthmatters.blog.gov.uk/2020/12/21/new-data-reveals-how-our-diets-are-changing-over-time/

https://www.bhf.org.uk/informationsupport/heart-matters-magazine/nutrition/5-a-day/colourful-foods

https://www.cancerresearchuk.org/about-cancer/causes-of-cancer/alcohol-and-cancer/does-alcohol-cause-cancer

https://www.cdc.gov/chronicdisease/resources/publications/factsheets/nutrition

https://www.cdc.gov/obesity/data/adult.html

https://www.eatforhealth.gov.au/guidelines/australian-guide-healthy-eating

https://food-guide.canada.ca/en/

https://www.gov.uk/government/publications/the-eatwell-guide

https://www.myplate.gov/

https://www.nationalgeographic.com/books/article/5-blue-zones-where-the-worlds-healthiest-people-live

https://www.nhs.uk/conditions/obesity/

https://www.rand.org/content/dam/rand/pubs/research_reports/RR4300/RR4379/RAND_RR4379.pdf

https://www.wcrf.org/dietandcancer/eat-wholegrains-vegetables-fruit-and-beans/

https://www.who.int/news-room/fact-sheets/detail/healthy-diet

Knight-Sepulveda K, Kais S, Santaolalla R, Abreu MT. Diet and Inflammatory Bowel Disease. *Gastroenterol Hepatol (N Y)*. 2015;11(8):511–520.

Linshan Li, Ronald B. Pegg, Ronald R. Eitenmiller, Ji-Yeon Chun, Adrian L. Kerrihard.

Selected nutrient analyses of fresh, fresh-stored, and frozen fruits and vegetables.

Journal of Food Composition and Analysis. 2017;59:8–17.

Piano MR. Alcohol's Effects on the Cardiovascular System. *Alcohol Res*. 2017;38(2):219–241.

Shreiner AB, Kao JY, Young VB. The Gut Microbiome in Health and in Disease. *Curr Opin Gastroenterol*. 2015;31(1):69–75.

Smith AP and Rogers R. Positive effects of a healthy snack (fruit) versus an unhealthy snack (chocolate/crisps) on subjective reports of mental and physical health: a preliminary intervention study. *Frontiers in Nutrition*. 2014;1:1–10.

Strandwitz P. Neurotransmitter modulation by the gut microbiota. *Brain Res*. 2018;1693(Pt B):128–133.

Topiwala A, Ebmeiner KP, Maullin-Sapey T, Nichols TE. No Safe Level of Alcohol Consumption for Brain Health: Observational Study of 25, 378 UK Biobank Participants. *MedRxiv* (2021) 2021.05.10.21256931.

Valdes AM, Walter J, Segal E, Spector TD. Role of the Gut Microbiota in Nutrition and Health. *BMJ*. 2018;361:k2179.

Wieërs G, Belkhir L, Enaud R, Leclercq S, Philippart de Foy JM, Dequenne I, de Timary P, Cani PD. How Probiotics Affect the Microbiota. *Front Cell Infect Microbiol*. 2020 Jan 15;9:454.

Wu X, Wu Y, He L, Wu L, Wang X, Liu Z. Effects of the intestinal microbial metabolite butyrate on the development of colorectal cancer. *J Cancer*. 2018;9(14):2510–2517.

Von Seck P, Martin Sander F, Lanzendorf L, von Seck S, Schmidt-Lucke A, Zielonka M, Schmidt-Lucke C. Persistent Weight Loss with a Non-Invasive Novel Medical Device to Change Eating Behaviour in

Obese Individuals with High rRsk Cardiovascular Risk Profile. *PLoS One*. 2017;12(4):e017458.

Environment

Andersen L, Corazon SSS, Stigsdotter UKK. Nature Exposure and Its Effects on Immune System Functioning: A Systematic Review. *Int J Environ Res Public Health*. 2021;18(4):1416.

Bellis MA, Sharp CA, Hughes K, Davies AR. Digital Overuse and Addictive Traits and Their Relationship With Mental Wellbeing and Socio-Demographic Factors: A National Population Survey for Wales. *Front Public Health*. 2021 9:585715.

Brailovskaia J, Margraf J. What does media use reveal about personality and mental health? An exploratory investigation among German students. *PLoS One*. 2018 13(1):e0191810.

Chen, H.-T.; Yu, C.-P.; Lee, H.-Y. The Effects of Forest Bathing on Stress Recovery: Evidence from Middle-Aged Females of Taiwan. *Forests*. 2018, 9, 403.

Domingues-Montanari S. Clinical and psychological effects of excessive screen time on children. *J Paediatr Child Health*. 2017 53(4):333–338.

Furuyashiki A, Tabuchi K, Norikoshi K, Kobayashi T, Oriyama S. A comparative study of the physiological and psychological effects of forest bathing (Shinrin-yoku) on working age people with and without depressive tendencies. *Environ Health Prev Med*. 2019 24(1):46.

Gaisberger M, Šanović R, Dobias H, Kolarž P, Moder A, Thalhamer J, Selimović A, Huttegger I, Ritter M, Hartl A. Effects of ionized waterfall aerosol on pediatric allergic asthma. *J Asthma*. 2012 49(8):830–8.

Han JW, Choi H, Jeon YH, Yoon CH, Woo JM, Kim W. The Effects of Forest Therapy on Coping with Chronic Widespread Pain: Physiological and Psychological Differences between Participants in a

Forest Therapy Program and a Control Group. *Int J Environ Res Public Health*. 2016 13(3):255.

Hassan A, Tao J, Li G, Jiang M, Aii L, Zhihui J, Zongfang L, Qibing C. Effects of Walking in Bamboo Forest and City Environments on Brainwave Activity in Young Adults. *Evid Based Complement Alternat Med*. 2018 Feb 11;2018:9653857.

Horiuchi M, Endo J, Takayama N, Murase K, Nishiyama N, Saito H, Fujiwara A. Impact of viewing vs. not viewing a real forest on physiological and psychological responses in the same setting. *Int J Environ Res Public Health*. 2014 11(10):10883–901.

https://nt.global.ssl.fastly.net/documents/sleep-mood-and-coastal-walking—-a-report-by-eleanor-ratcliffe.pdf

https://www.ofcom.org.uk/about-ofcom/latest/features-and-news/decade-of-digital-dependency

Ideno Y, Hayashi K, Abe Y, Ueda K, Iso H, Noda M, Lee JS, Suzuki S. Blood pressure-lowering effect of *Shinrin-yoku* (Forest bathing): a systematic review and meta-analysis. *BMC Complementary and Alternative Medicine*. 2017 17(409).

Im SG, Choi H, Jeon YH, Song MK, Kim W, Woo JM. Comparison of Effect of Two-Hour Exposure to Forest and Urban Environments on Cytokine, Anti-Oxidant, and Stress Levels in Young Adults. *Int J Environ Res Public Health*. 2016 13(7):625.

Kobayashi H, Song C, Ikei H, Park BJ, Kagawa T, Miyazaki Y. Combined Effect of Walking and Forest Environment on Salivary Cortisol Concentration. *Front Public Health*. 2019 7:376.

Kobayashi H, Song C, Ikei H, Park BJ, Lee J, Kagawa T, Miyazaki Y. Forest Walking Affects Autonomic Nervous Activity: A Population-Based Study. *Front Public Health*. 2018 6:278.

Kobayashi H, Song C, Ikei H, Kagawa T, Miyazaki Y. Analysis of Individual Variations in Autonomic Responses to Urban and Forest Environments. *Evid Based Complement Alternat Med*. 2015;2015:671094.

Lee I, Choi H, Bang KS, Kim S, Song M, Lee B. Effects of Forest Therapy on Depressive Symptoms among Adults: A Systematic Review. *Int J Environ Res Public Health*. 2017 14(3):321.

Li Q, Morimoto K, Nakadai A, Inagaki H, Katsumata M, Shimizu T, Hirata Y, Hirata K, Suzuki H, Miyazaki Y, Kagawa T, Koyama Y, Ohira T, Takayama N, Krensky AM, Kawada T. Forest bathing enhances human natural killer activity and expression of anti-cancer proteins. *Int J Immunopathol Pharmacol*. 2007 20(2 Suppl 2):3–8.

Linares C, Sellier AL. How bad is the mere presence of a phone? A replication of Przybylski and Weinstein (2013) and an extension to creativity. *PLoS One*. 2021 16(6):e0251451.

McEwan K, Giles D, Clarke FJ, Kotera Y, Evans G, Terebenina O, Minou L, Teeling C, Basran J, Wood W, Weil D. A Pragmatic Controlled Trial of Forest Bathing Compared with Compassionate Mind Training in the UK: Impacts on Self-Reported Wellbeing and Heart Rate Variability. *Sustainability*. 2021 13(3):1380.

Mehta R, Zhu RJ. Blue or red? Exploring the effect of color on cognitive task performances. *Science*. 2009 323(5918):1226–9.

Morita E, Fukuda S, Nagano J, Hamajima N, Yamamoto H, Iwai Y, Nakashima T, Ohira H, Shirakawa T. Psychological effects of forest environments on healthy adults: Shinrin-yoku (forest-air bathing, walking) as a possible method of stress reduction. *Public Health*. 2007 Jan;121(1):54–63.

Nutsford D, Pearson AL, Kingham S, Reitsma F. Residential exposure to visible blue space (but not green space) associated with lower psychological distress in a capital city. *Health Place*. 2016 39:70-8.

Orben A, Przybylski AK. The association between adolescent wellbeing and digital technology use. *Nat Hum Behav*. 2019 3(2):173–182.

Peterfalvi A, Meggyes M, Makszin L, Farkas N, Miko E, Miseta A, Szereday L. Forest Bathing Always Makes Sense: Blood Pressure-Lowering and Immune System-Balancing Effects in Late Spring and

Winter in Central Europe. *Int J Environ Res Public Health*. 2021 18(4):2067.

Przybylski AK, Weinstein N. A Large-Scale Test of the Goldilocks Hypothesis. *Psychol Sci*. 2017 28(2):204–215.

Shin WS, Shin CS, Yeoun PS, Kim JJ. The influence of interaction with forest on cognitive function, *Scandinavian Journal of Forest Research*. 2011 26:6, 595–598.

Twenge JM, Campbell WK. Media Use Is Linked to Lower Psychological Wellbeing: Evidence from Three Datasets. *Psychiatr Q*. 2019 90(2):311–331.

Wen Y, Yan Q, Pan Y, Gu X, Liu Y. Medical empirical research on forest bathing (Shinrin-yoku): a systematic review. *Environ Health Prev Med*. 2019 24(1):70.

Yu CP, Lin CM, Tsai MJ, Tsai YC, Chen CY. Effects of Short Forest Bathing Program on Autonomic Nervous System Activity and Mood States in Middle-Aged and Elderly Individuals. *Int J Environ Res Public Health*. 2017 14(8):897.

Relationships and Social Connections

Baumeister RF, Leary MR. The need to belong: desire for interpersonal attachments as a fundamental human motivation. *Psychol Bull*. 1995 117(3):497-529.

Eisenberger NI. The neural bases of social pain: evidence for shared representations with physical pain. *Psychosom Med*. 2012 74(2):126–135.

Holt-Lunstad J, Smith TB, Baker M, Harris T, Stephenson D. Loneliness and social isolation as risk factors for mortality: a meta-analytic review. *Perspect Psychol Sci*. 2015 10(2):227–37.

https://www.ons.gov.uk/peoplepopulationandcommunity/wellbeing/articles/measuringnationalwellbeing/2016

Maslow, AH. A Theory of Human Motivation. Psychological Review 1943 50:370–396.

Principles of Cognitive Neuroscience 2008 Ed Purves D *et al*, Pub Sinauer Associates; 1st edition (12 Feb. 2008).

Goals and Habits

Clear J. *Atomic Habits*. Penguin Random House; 2018.

Lally P and Gardner B. Promoting Habit Formation. *Health Psychology Review*. 2013. 7:sup1;ppS137-S158.

Maas J, de Ridder DT, de Vet E. Do Distant Foods Reduce Intake? The Effect of Food Accessibility on Consumption. *Psychol Health. 2012.* 27(Suppl. 2): 59–73.

Ideas, Mindset and Stress Reduction

Superwoman Syndrome

Shaevitz M. *The Superwoman Syndrome*. Warner Books; 1984.

Short Emma (ed.). *A Prescription for Healthy Living: A Guide to Lifestyle Medicine*. Elsevier; 2021.

Meditation and Mindfulness

Cahn BR, Polich J. Meditation states and traits: EEG, ERP, and neuroimaging studies.

Psychol Bull. 2006 132(2):180–211.

Davidson RJ, Kabat-Zinn J, Schumacher J, Rosenkranz M, Muller D, Santorelli SF, Urbanowski F, Harrington A, Bonus K, Sheridan JF. Alterations in brain and immune function produced by mindfulness. *Psychosom Med*. 2003 65(4):564–70.

Farias, M, Maraldi, E, Wallenkampf, KC, Lucchetti, G. Adverse events in meditation practices and meditation-based therapies: a systematic review. *Acta Psychiatrica Scandinavica*. 2020 142(5):374–393.

Goyal M, Singh S, Sibinga EMS, Gould NF, Rowland-Seymour A, Sharma R, Berger Z, Sleicher D, Maron DD, Shihab HM, Ranasinghe PD, Linn S, Saha S, Bass EB, Haythornthwaite JA. Meditation Programs for Psychological Stress and Wellbeing: A Systematic Review and Meta-analysis. *JAMA Intern Med*. 2014 174(3):357–368.

Hölzel BK, Carmody J, Vangel M, Congleton C, Yerramsetti SM, Gard T, Lazzar SW. Mindfulness practice leads to increases in regional brain gray matter density. *Psychiatry Res*. 2011 191(1):36–43.

Kaliman P, Álvarez-López MJ, Cosín-Tomás M, Rosenkranz MA, Lutz A, Davidson RJ. Rapid changes in histone deacetylases and inflammatory gene expression in expert meditators. *Psychoneuroendocrinology*. 2014 40:96–107.

Killingsworth MA, Gilbert DT. A wandering mind is an unhappy mind. *Science*. 2010 12;330(6006):932.

Lindhal JR, Fisher NE, Cooper DJ, Rosen RK, Britton WB. The varieties of contemplative experience: A mixed-methods study of challenges in Western Buddhists. *PLoS One*. 2017 24:12(5):e01762939.

Lomas T, Ivtzan I, Fu CH. A systematic review of the neurophysiology of mindfulness on EEG oscillations. *Neurosci Biobehav Rev*. 2015 57:401–10.

Mooneyham BW, Schooler JW. The costs and benefits of mind-wandering: a review. *Can J Exp Psychol*. 2013 67(1):11–18.

Ponte Márquez PH, Feliu-Soler A, Solé-Villa MJ, Matas-Pericas L, Filella-Agullo D, Ruiz-Herrerias M, Soler-Ribaudi J, Roca-Cusachs Coll A, Arroyo-Díaz JA. Benefits of mindfulness meditation in reducing blood pressure and stress in patients with arterial hypertension. *J Hum Hypertens*. 2019 33(3):237–247.

Schneider RH, Grim CE, Rainforth MV, Kotchen T, Nidich SI, Gaylord-King C, Salerno JW, Kotchen JM, Alexander CN. Stress reduction in the secondary prevention of cardiovascular disease: randomized, controlled trial of transcendental meditation and health education in Blacks. *Circ Cardiovasc Qual Outcomes*. 2012 5(6):750–8.

Zeidan F, Martucci KT, Kraft RA, Gordon NS, McHaffie JG, Coghill RC. Brain Mechanisms Supporting the Modulation of Pain by Mindfulness. *Meditation Journal of Neuroscience*. 2011 31(14); 5540–5548.

Gratitude

Emmons R, McCullough M. Counting blessings versus burdens: an experimental investigation of gratitude and subjective wellbeing in daily life. *J Pers Soc Psychol*. 2003 84:377e89.

Emmons R. How gratitude can help you through hard times. 2013 [Online], https://greatergood.berkeley.edu/article/item/how_gratitude_can_hel p_you_through_hard_times.

Achor S. *The happiness advantage*. S.l. New York: The Crown Publishing Group; 2010. p. 98.

Kindness

Alden LE and Trew JL. If it makes you happy: engaging in kind acts increases positive affect in socially anxious individuals. *Emotion*. 2013 13(1):64–75.

Aristotle (translated by Lee Honeycutt). Kindness. Rhetoric, Book 2, Chapter 7. Archived from the original on December 13, 2004.

Chancellor J, Margolis S, Jacobs Bao K and Lyubomirsky, S. Everyday prosociality in the workplace: The reinforcing benefits of giving, getting, and glimpsing. *Emotion*. 2018 18(4): 507–517.

Dunn EW, Aknin LB, Norton MI. Spending money on others promotes happiness. *Science*. 2008 319(5870):1687–8.

Erard M and Matacie C. Did Kindness Prime our Species for Language? *Science*. 2018 361(6401): 436–437.

Hamlin JK, Wynn K, Bloom P. Social evaluation by preverbal infants. *Nature*. 2007 450(7169):557-9. doi: 10.1038/nature06288. PMID: 18033298.

https://www.campaigntoendloneliness.org/the-facts-on-loneliness/

https://dictionary.cambridge.org/dictionary/english/kindness

http://www.macmillandictionaryblog.com/kindness

https://www.mind.org.uk/information-support/types-of-mental-health-problems/statistics-and-facts-about-mental-health/how-common-are-mental-health-problems/#.Xg7pXZP7TOQ

https://www.relate.org.uk/about-us/media-centre/press-releases/2017/2/22/loneliness-rising-1-8-adults-have-no-close-friends

https://www.theguardian.com/society/2019/nov/05/welfare-changes-key-factor-rising-poverty-food-bank-use-study-finds

https://thepsychologist.bps.org.uk/volume-31/february-2018/kindness-societys-golden-chain

https://www.trusselltrust.org/news-and-blog/latest-stats/end-year-stats/

https://www.who.int/mental_health/evidence/burn-out/en/

Kim SK and Ferraro KF. Do Productive Activities Reduce Inflammation in Later Life? Multiple Roles, Frequency of Activities and C-Reactive Protein. *The Gerontologist*. 2013 54(5): 830–839.

Klaber RE and Bailey S. Kindness: an underrated currency. *BMJ*. 2019 367:l6099.

Nelson SK, Layous K, Cole SW, Lyubomirsky S. Do unto others or treat yourself? The effects of prosocial and self-focused behaviour on psychological flourishing. *Emotion*. 2016 16(6): 850–61.

Sleep

Short Emma (ed.). *A Prescription for Healthy Living: A Guide to Lifestyle Medicine*. Elsevier; 2021.

Besedovsky L et al. The Sleep-Immune Crosstalk in Health and Disease. *Physiol Rev*. 2019 99(3):1325–1380.

Besedovsky L et al. Sleep and immune function. *Pflugers Arch*. 2012 463(1):121-137.

Bjorness TE and Greene RW. Adenosine and sleep. *Curr Neuropharmacol*. 2009 7(3):238–245.

Fismer KL and Pilkington K. Lavender and sleep: a systematic review of the evidence. *European Journal of Integrative Medicine*. 2012 4(4):e436-e447.

Gnocchi D and Bruscalupi G. Circadian Rhythms and Hormonal Homeostasis: Pathophysiological Implications. *Biology*. (Basel) 2017 6(1):10.

https://www.formulatehealth.com/blog/insomnia-statistics-uk-how-many-people-have-sleep-problems

Kline CE. The bidirectional relationship between exercise and sleep: Implications for exercise adherence and sleep improvement. *Am J Lifestyle Med*. 2014 8(6):375–379.

Leproult R and Van Cauter E. Role of sleep and sleep loss in hormonal release and metabolism. *Endocr Dev*. 2010 17:11–21.

Patterson F et al. Sleep as a Target for Optimized Response to Smoking Cessation Treatment. *Nicotine & Tobacco Research*. 2019 21(2):139–148.

Vandekerckhove M and Wang YL. Emotion, emotion regulation and sleep: An intimate relationship. *AIMS Neurosci*. 2017 5(1):1–17.

Xie L et al. Sleep drives metabolite clearance from the adult brain. *Science*. 2013 342(6156):373–377.